SOUL SURGERY

The Ultimate Self-Healing

Text and Workbook

by

Richard Jafolla

DeVorss & Company
P.O. Box 550
Marina del Rey, California 90291

ISBN: 0-87516-473-0
Library of Congress Card Catalog Number: 81-71018

Printed in the United States of America

CONTENTS

PART I — TEXT

PART II — WORKBOOK

ALL THINGS ARE POSSIBLE

SOUL SURGERY

Part One

THE TEXT

INTRODUCTION TO THE TEXT

"I just don't understand it! What's happening to me? I've tried positive thinking, positive prayer, positive everything! I've begged God for help. I've used every healing principle I know. And *still* this problem keeps hanging on. Won't I ever be rid of it? Will I have it forever? What am I doing wrong? Why won't it go away?"

Is this you? Is there one problem looming menacingly in your life, overshadowing all others? A problem which has brazenly resisted every attempt to conquer it? A problem of such unyielding tenacity and long duration that you wonder if it will ever stop tyrannizing you?

It could even be that your problem is relatively new—one which has recently exploded into your life and whose crushing impact has scattered its debris on you so pervasively that you feel you must dig out from under it before it smothers you any further.

This extraordinary problem, whatever its tenure, could be a physical challenge like heart disease, cancer or arthritis. Or it could be something you have allowed to gain dominion over you through an overdependence upon it, such as alcohol, tobacco or even food! Maybe the problem is a personal relationship which you are unable to reconcile. Or perhaps your challenge lies in the area of prosperity. Poverty, after all, is a state of mind which can be self-perpetuating if you allow it to become so. Whatever problem confronts you, if it is one which you have not been able to purge from your life, then this problem is an exceptional one and must be dealt with in an exceptional way, not only because of the obvious discomfort that it is causing but, more importantly, because any persistent unwanted pain—either physiological or psychological—is merely the outward manifestation of an obstruction which lies deep within your own soul. The more resistant to any treatment the problem has been, the more deeply hidden is its root. And the deeper that root is hidden, the more subtly it is able to restrict the natural flow and expression of such things as love, health, abundance, freedom and happiness into and out of your soul. For this reason alone—that it is inhibiting your true self expression—*the root of your problem must be excised from your soul forever!*

But the problem has not responded to normal treatment. You have tried everything you can think of and still it persists! This indicates the need for a more radical strategy. The excision of such a deeply-rooted problem will need a very special kind of procedure, one that will assure that the removal is complete and permanent leaving no pain, no scars and no remorse.

There *is* such a procedure. There is a technique which can remove the problem from your life completely and permanently and it is the purpose of this book not only to enumerate the steps involved in this procedure, but to guide you and inspire you as you take each step.

The procedure is called SOUL SURGERY. By utilizing the special techniques of SOUL SURGERY you will be able to free yourself from any situation you feel is inhibiting your full expression. But since the root of the problem lies deep within you and only *you* know where it is, the surgery can be successful only if it is *self*-administered. Often, someone truly interested in your well-being, like a spiritual counselor or a very special friend, can be of valuable assistance. Books and articles, too, can help to point you in the proper direction as can listening to instructive tapes and attending inspiring lectures. But in the final analysis, if you are to fully express the divine destiny of your existence, it is *you and you alone* who must make the decision, make the "incision" and remove the constricting condition from your life once and for all. *Only you can perform your own SOUL SURGERY because only you are familiar enough with the anatomy of your own soul.*

SOUL SURGERY, utilizing the physical, mental and spiritual laws which direct your life, changes your awareness, attitudes and actions so that you can remove any unwanted condition which you feel is inhibiting the full expression of your innate divinity.

SOUL SURGERY is easy to understand, easy to utilize and adapts smoothly and naturally to any lifestyle. It has changed the lives of many people. It can change yours.

Chapter I

THREE-PART HARMONY

When we are balanced in spirit, soul and body, nothing can affect our spiritual, emotional or physical equilibrium.

Before studying the seven steps involved in SOUL SURGERY it is important that we have a clear understanding of just what the soul is and why it is essential that it be kept free of any encumbrances. However, we cannot study the aspects of the soul without first discussing the three-fold nature of man with its three distinct attributes—spirit, soul and body. These phases are separate yet they are coexistent. To the extent that we emphasize one we diminish the others. A balance is necessary, an equilibrium essential, if we are to fully express our divine design. We must engage in a dynamic interplay between these three phases so that they remain equal in expression. When we have attained this trilateral symmetry we are centered and poised. But when one or two phases are allowed to dominate we lose our center, we become "eccentric" and unable to keep our lives on course.

1

Consider the universe. The planets, stars, galaxies and constellations whirl through the heavens in a persistent splendor. Each has its own orbit. Each is affected by the proximity, mass and speed of the others. As long as this dynamic balance is maintained, each planet remains safe from collision. But what happens if somehow the speed or mass or proximity of one planet is changed? The orbit of the planet will become eccentric and eventually a collision will occur. The collision will not have been caused by a wrathful Creative Power's suspension of any laws. Quite the contrary. When the dynamic balance is destroyed, eccentricity is inevitable and collision *must* ensue because the planets will scrupulously follow universal laws laid down by a scrupulously just Creator.

Such must be the case in our lives. A crucial balance, a special interplay must be sought so that spirit, soul and body will remain equal and our involvement in the world about us will be calm, poised and centered. Our actions will not be dictated by what happens *to* us—that is a *re*-action—but will instead spring from the infinite well of universal love which resides deep within our self, deep within our very spirit, and flows out through our soul to manifest as the individualized expression of the Eternal Spirit—God—which is each of us. When we are balanced in spirit, soul and body we are centered in God—in Good —and nothing can affect our spiritual, emotional or physical equilibrium.

SPIRIT

In order for us to express our perfection there must be a constant source of inspiration available to us, a well from which we can draw, a pattern from which we can copy.

Spirit is that ultimate fountainhead of inspiration. It is the infinite well. It is the perfect pattern. Spirit does not bother with effects or impressions because *it is the source of all*, including soul and body.

The eternal, unchanging nucleus of us, the absolute essence of what we are, is our spirit. We call this spiritual nature our "perfect center" or our "Christ-center." It is who and what we *really* are. It is our individuality, our only *true* self, not the self which is imbued with ego and struts through life reacting to impressions from its surroundings. It forever "is." It cannot be destroyed. It is infinite, immutable and indestructable.

From spirit flow all of the divine ideas of God-Mind. The flow is unceasing since the Source is infinite. But we can utilize only as much as our soul is capable of comprehending and accepting. A well may bubble up an unlimited abundance of water but we can utilize only the amount we can fit into the container we have brought to the well. Thus spirit presents us with an unlimited abundance of health and wholeness, for example. But if we feel "unworthy" of perfect health, if we believe we have inherited our malady, if our consciousness dwells only on sickness, then we will be unable to accept our gift. Our feelings and beliefs, our "sick consciousness" will effectively block our wholeness. Our "container"—our soul—will be too cluttered and will be unable to receive our complete good. Spirit gives us infinite inspiration but we can utilize only the amount which our soul can contain, i.e., which our consciousness can accept.

SOUL

The soul, or mind, is our consciousness. It is the sum total of all that we have accepted from the spirit or Christ mind, which is our superconscious. The soul is the *user* of the ideas of God which flow from the superconscious. But the soul can only use what it is capable of laying claim to and since the soul is our *individual* awareness of our existence, each of us can utilize his spirit only to the extent of his own *self*-awareness.

The realm of the soul embraces the entire mind—both the conscious mind where thinking is carried out and the subconscious mind where feeling and remembering occur. Therefore, not only can the expression of the spirit through the soul be inhibited by our everyday thoughts, opinions and feelings, but it can also be affected by the many accumulated race ideas and beliefs from the past. If we are to allow spirit to flow through us we must remove anything that will inhibit that flow. Spirit is always giving, is always flowing, but spirit must be allowed to flow unhampered by the false beliefs that adhere to our soul.

We sometimes allow the belief in poverty to restrain the flow of God's abundance through us. We might allow the belief in hate and evil to pervert the flow of God's love through us. We often allow the belief in sickness and death to obstruct the flow of God's life force through us. These are the barnacles of false belief which must be scraped off our souls so that we can be more responsive to the spiritual currents which urge us toward our good.

Yet it is so easy to accumulate these delusive doctrines. Our senses are constantly assaulted with suggestions of limitation. A mother may innocently tell her child, "The doctor says you will have to take this medicine because *you have bad sinuses just like your father*." So the seed is planted, the barnacle is attached, the maxim accepted. Instead of believing the truth that we are all expressions of a perfect Creator, inheriting only life and wholeness, the child begins believing that he has a limitation.

We see and hear on the television what to do for *"your* arthritis," *"your* headache," *"your* constipation." We come to believe that we can possess these things and before long we do possess them. We make references such as *"my* arthritis," *"my* headaches," or *"my"* constipation." Then what we possess begins to possess us. The maxim we have innocently allowed into our soul has now turned malignant. It has been given a reality and power of its own. It is no longer an abstraction in the outer world. We have allowed it to enter the inner sanctum of our soul—of our mind—and, having done so, it has become part of us.

If left untreated this malignancy will impede and retard any spiritual stream of truth. The longer it is allowed to remain the more it will grow. And the more it grows the more obstructive it will become. *These malignant maxims must be removed from our soul.* When the soul or mind is clear and poised in its true spiritual *milieu* the body can only be whole and healthy. Healing the body is secondary to healing the soul. In fact, healing any outer condition— whether it be poverty, fear, unsatisfactory personal relationships, lack of love or any of the myriad other self-generated problems we are prone to—is secondary to healing the soul.

Soul Pivotal

The soul is the pivotal phase of man. It not only touches the inner sanctum of spirit from which it receives pure inspiration, but it also touches the external world of appearances where it receives impressions from the five senses. And just imagine how many false impressions we have allowed ourselves to accept! From the time we are able to understand, we are constantly bombarded with words, deeds and impressions which express the strongly held beliefs of not only our immediate family, but the race of man in general.

We may be told when we are tiny children that black people or white people or yellow people are inferior to us. We are often taught that God comes only to our church on Sunday. We might be warned that ''diabetes runs in our family.'' We may be reminded that ''the rich get richer and the poor get poorer.'' Thus are sown the seeds of hate, intolerance and fear, the belief in sickness and poverty and all the other false ideas which can so easily attach themselves to our soul.

Inspiration or Impression?

One night of television watching or the reading of a few popular magazines or newspapers will very subtly show us just what some other of these popularly accepted beliefs are. Advertising agencies spend much money to determine just what the majority of the population desires and fears and what their strongly held beliefs are. Their advertisements are then geared to feed off of those beliefs in order to sell merchandise. And how do they word their clever ads? We hear things like, ''Now that the flu season is here it's time to take some . . . ,'' (as if there is a capricious Creative Power who inflicts us with bad seasons). Or even more subtly, ''Now that you're thirty-five you don't have as much energy so you should take some . . . ,'' (as if going around the sun thirty-five times has anything to do with the way we feel). Or we are told that ''When you put your money in a . . . account it's safe,'' (as if the unlimited abundance from a Limitless Source can only be safe in a bank vault!).

Our fears are orchestrated for us daily as we watch the news and read the newspaper. And most of us are satisfied to dance to this discordant symphony. But such a cacophony, based as it is on mere appearances, can only fill our soul with disharmony and anxiety. If we listen to it, it will effectively muffle the inspiring sound of the different drummer deep within us which is calling us to march to the harmonious tempo of Truth.

"But what does it matter what I listen to?" we may ask. "My trouble is in my outer world—my body and my affairs—not my soul!" This brings us to the third phase of man's being.

BODY

There must be a vehicle through which spirit and soul can express. Such a vehicle is the body. It is the physical organism through which they can both manifest in the world of form. Spirit, of course, must express through soul but as we have already seen the soul is pivotal. The soul can receive pure and perfect *inspiration* from God through the unlimited spirit phase or it can receive adulterated, impaired *impressions* from the outer world through the limited five senses. Since the body is the outer expression of the soul, *the health of the body and its outer affairs is in direct proportion to the "health" of the soul.* When the soul is directed away from sense impressions and toward divine ideas flowing through it from spirit, the body and outer affairs become perfect just as spirit is perfect. There can be no sickness, disease, pain or suffering. There can be no hatred, fear, anxiety or lack. There can be none of these because these states do not exist in perfect spirit! But when the soul re-directs its attention *away* from divine ideas and toward the impressions gleaned from our limited five senses, then we can receive only a limited input and our body and outer affairs suffer. The body is the projection of our idea of what it *should* be. The condition of our body and our lives always exactly mirrors the character of our thought—of our soul.

In its original creation, as an idea in God-Mind, the body is perfect. It must be perfect because it is conceived out of a perfect Mind. It does not originate as an organism of flesh, it originates as a perfect idea. While it is perfect in concept it may take on appearances that are less than perfect according to the use *we* make of this idea. The body will become the sum total of what we believe about it.

Michelangelo's magnificent sculpture *David* began as an inspiration in the sculptor's mind. Before he ever touched chisel to stone the perfect *David* existed in that block of marble. Of course an infinite amount of other forms also existed but to Michelangelo's consciousness there was one IDEAL *David* in the marble and he chipped away all the extraneous matter until it emerged. The *David* that he created perfectly mirrors his consciousness at the time he did it. It reflects his thoughts, feelings, impressions and race beliefs which he had up until then. Thus Michelangelo is the soul of *David*. He did not totally "create" him, for in fact *David* always existed as an *idea*, but it was Michelangelo —using the character of his own thoughts, expressing his own consciousness—who formed the *David* to mirror those thoughts and that consciousness.

Analogies are never perfect, but in much the same way our soul takes the perfect idea of man in God-Mind and "sculptures" spiritual substance into a body which exactly mirrors the character of our thoughts—of our own consciousness. When our consciousness is aligned with God-Mind and is receiving inspiration from the spirit, spiritual substance is formed into a perfect body. However, the body will deviate from perfection to the *exact* extent that our soul is inhibited from expressing God's inspiration. The body and the affairs of the body are always a perfect expression of the soul. *ALWAYS!*

Chapter II

THE ROLE OF THE SOUL

I am the master of my fate:
I am the captain of my soul.

"Invictus"—W.E. Henley

The soul is the crucial area in dealing with any aspect of our lives which we deem unsatisfactory. Spirit, of course, is perfect and will never change for it is part of perfect, changeless God-Mind. However, in order to manifest that perfection in our body and affairs, spirit must flow through soul. We know that as long as our thoughts are directed to spirit, the flow of inspiration through our soul is infinite. There can be no needs, no desires, no disappointments, no apprehensions, no fears, no lack—nothing but total satisfaction. When we are centered in spirit we are drinking from the *only* waters which can quench our eternal thirst. As it flows unimpeded through our soul the perfect *idea* of body in Divine-Mind is brought forth as perfect *expression* of body.

Whereas the spirit of man can only "know," the soul of man is capable of thinking, feeling and remembering. We can receive our inspiration from our spirit—from pure "knowing"—or we can turn toward the world of appearances and receive impressions. We can think, we can feel, we can remember. Or, we can "know." The choice is ours. We exercise our free-will and we choose.

"JUDGE NOT BY APPEARANCES . . ."

The senses are imperfect sentinels with which to judge *true* values. Man himself has invented cameras which can "see" better than eyes, microphones which can "hear" better than ears, machines which can "touch" better than skin, exotic computers which can "taste" better than a tongue and electro-chemical devices which can "smell" better than a nose. In the unbelievably vast electromagnetic spectrum between ultra-short cosmic waves of one trillionth of a centimeter in length and immensely long radio waves of thousands of miles in length, we are visually limited to seeing only the extremely narrow band of wave lengths between ultra-violet and infra-red—a range of only three-one hundred thousandths of a centimeter! All else is out of our physical capability to detect! How can we rely on information gleaned from such limited gauges as our five senses?

When we allow ourselves to judge by our five senses, we run the risk of cluttering the soul with the debris of appearances. Too often we allow these appearances to ripen into impressions and blossom into our lives as beliefs. These beliefs easily attach themselves to hidden corners of our soul and there grow so quietly that we assume that they have always been there and that they are an integral part of us. Each time we feel lacking when we "see" in the newspaper that inflation is affecting our prosperity; each time we are enveloped by a chilling fear of helplessness when we "touch" that lump on our breast; each time we become apprehensive when we "hear" from our diabetic parents that diabetes is often an inherited disease, we have given dominion to a limited sense impression. It is these hidden false beliefs which easily fester and grow if allowed to stay. They become larger each time we give dominion to them, each time they are allowed to express. And in growing they form areas of blockage in the soul which restrict and impede the free flow from spirit. Our body and outer affairs, then, reflect this restriction and we are unable to express spirit fully and completely.

Feelings of lack, thoughts of fear, apprehensions about the future—any of these erroneous attitudes which we possess—stealthily creep into our lives and begin to gain power over us. That which we have given power to soon possesses us. We begin *re*acting from the perspective of a sense-being instead of *acting* from the sense of a divine being. We become like players in a drama, taking our cues from the audience instead of following the directions of the playwright. And so we come to believe that our prosperity can be affected by an erratic stock market, forgetting that our true prosperity can never be affected by anything but our most closely held thoughts about it. We come to believe that part of our body will tolerate deadly tissues, forgetting that the malignancy is not in the tissues but in the belief itself! We come to believe that we can inherit a disease, forgetting that our only *true* inheritance is from a perfect Creator.

These limitations, of course, must be removed so that our bodies and affairs can become whole again. All the false beliefs must be excised from the soul so that they don't restrict our good from flowing through us. The soul must be made clean, pure, smooth and free of any growths which will encumber it. This is usually done simply by becoming aware of the need to change and then redirecting our thoughts and actions to realign ourselves with the Universal Mind. In this way we can rid our mind of most of the false beliefs which we have allowed to restrict us.

But what of those nagging erroneous beliefs which won't let go, the ones that we emotionally cling to, the ones which have taken on the sanctity of "dogma?" In spite of all that our intellect tells us about their being false, we cannot seem to shake them. They fester and grow, fed by our constant use of them in our daily activities. These are the tenacious tumors that will require SOUL SURGERY for complete removal and for our ultimate self-healing.

We Control Our Good

Any growth of limitation festering on our soul will successfully restrict all of the abundance surrounding us. God pours His infinite blessings upon us but our soul must be open to receive them. For example, a belief in poverty will hide our prosperity from us. It will blind us to the fact that God's gifts are for the taking, that prosperity abounds, that we have only to free our consciousness from the false belief of limitation to feast at God's overflowing table. However, when this blindfold of false belief is removed we will come to see that we exist in an infinitely prosperous universe and that as part of that universe we are privy to *all* that it contains. We will no longer live in fear of "lack;" instead we will have complete faith in God as our constant source of supply.

But here is the best part. When this blinding belief in poverty is eliminated, other aspects of our life will also prosper! To our mind we will have sought only prosperity. But in fact the removal of the limiting belief from our soul will have opened us up to receive not only more prosperity but also more health, more faith, more love, more happiness, more of *all* of the other gifts of God.

A consciousness which dwells on poverty restricts growth in *every* area, not just finances. A consciousness which dwells on sickness restricts growth in *every* area, not just health. A consciousness which dwells on fear restricts growth in *every* area, not just faith. When any false belief is removed, the flow of all of God's gifts changes from a dribble to a deluge and *all* aspects of our lives change.

Chapter III

THE OPERATION

The symptom of the problem is what is manifesting in our life, but the problem itself is in our soul.

With SOUL SURGERY we are in the unique position of being at one and the same time both "surgeon" and "patient." We are operating on ourselves! This has many advantages, the foremost of which is that of allowing us to control all aspects of our self-healing. If we feel that the removal of a false belief or a long-accepted creed is too painful or is proceeding too quickly, we can slow down or temporarily stop the process and give our body and our affairs time to adjust.

Also, when we operate on ourselves, when we change our own consciousness, we know that the change will be permanent. Too often a "healing" is merely transient because the false belief that is causing it is only temporarily suppressed by someone else's effort coupled with our vague desire. When the other person withdraws his assistance we are left feeling alone and helpless again. The suppressed belief re-declares itself and our problem re-appears. Thus the inspiring preaching at a healing meeting, the moving music, the evocative use of the name of Jesus Christ, the powerful testimonials of others who have been healed all combine to change the consciousness of the one in need of a healing. The false belief which caused the health problem is suppressed and he is healed! But after leaving the service, he no longer has anyone to help him sustain this expanded consciousness and so that false belief, which was merely suppressed, slowly reasserts itself and the malady slowly returns. If the false belief is never completely purged this is inevitable. It will always reassert itself sooner or later, either as the same dis-ease or as a different one.

However, when we have performed our own SOUL SURGERY, we can be sure that every vestige of the false belief is excised and that none of the malignant maxim which had caused our plight remains to fester and grow and affect us again. Only *we* can be sure that it is removed forever.

It is important to know that in SOUL SURGERY we are not seeking "health" exclusively or "love" exclusively or "prosperity" exclusively. These are not separate entities floating around the universe as specific pieces of spiritual substance to be taken out of God's inventory and placed in our personal account. God's abundance is not measurable or divisible; it is individually infinite and expresses at the same time as health, as love, as prosperity, as joy, as ful-fillment, as all that is good and desirable. God is constantly giving and the gifts are free. We don't have to ask; *we have only to accept.*

SOUL SURGERY frees the soul of false beliefs and in doing so—in allowing God's gifts to pour into our lives—we are not asking for one specific thing. In fact, *we are not asking for anything!* We are merely allowing what is already ours to flow into our lives and affairs.

INSTRUCTIONS

The steps of SOUL SURGERY are deceptively simple. It is important to read each chapter carefully with an open mind and heart. Do not attempt to begin your SOUL SURGERY until you have completed the entire book. Then go back and begin applying each chapter to your specific challenge. Proceed deliberately. Be patient and do not hurry. The ultimate goal of a runner may be to compete in a twenty-six mile marathon. But even if he can't run that distance now, as long as he runs as far as he can each day, he will eventually become strong enough to run the desired distance. It is important to realize that, like the runner, as long as you are *striving* to improve you *are* improving. You may experience temporary setbacks or long periods when improvement does not seem to be evident, but these are often times when your consciousness is working hard to accept a new concept and so you must realize that as long as your thoughts are based on Truth, your consciousness will always eventually adopt these new ideas.

Be thorough. After reading all of the steps you may want to change the order, but be sure you thoroughly understand each step before going on to the next.

And lastly and most importantly, it is usually best to work alone. Do not share your personal SOUL SURGERY with anyone unless he is very close to you and is vitally interested in your spiritual well-being. The *symptom* of the problem is what is manifesting in your life but *the problem itself is in your soul.* The soul has special secrets and those secrets are for you alone to know. If you feel you must share them, be sure it is with someone who has your best interests at heart.

Remember, even when you work alone you are not alone. God is always with you. When you are performing your SOUL SURGERY you can be sure that God is in attendance, guiding you and helping you. A creator can only know itself through its creations. Your Creator wants you to succeed and you will succeed. He created you as perfect and He wants you to express that perfection. But God can't do *for* you, He can only do *with* you. God can only put His strength behind *your* effort.

With this important fact firmly in mind, let's go now to the first step of your self-healing.

Chapter IV

AWARENESS

We are sick or poor or lonely because sickness or poverty or loneliness is serving the purpose of our soul.

It is impossible to formulate a solution to a problem if there is not first an AWARENESS of a problem! The first step in overcoming any difficulty is to recognize that the difficulty does exist. Therefore, before anything at all can be remedied in our lives, we must first become *aware* that something exists which needs to be remedied!

If we were to set out from New York City wanting to drive to Maine but inadvertently began driving toward Florida, we would certainly have a problem. The further we drove the more serious our problem would become. But our only hope of remedying our predicament would be to first become aware that we had a problem. There could be no hope of remedy until we realized that we were driving south instead of north. Only when we became aware of the situation could we take any steps to change it. There could be no remedy without first a realization—an awareness.

If we feel that we are "bucking the current," then perhaps we should check to see if we are swimming in the wrong direction. If there is something in our lives which does not seem right—if we are not expressing abundant health or love or prosperity or fulfillment or happiness or all of our divine inheritance—then we must become aware that we have a problem. Something is restricting our full expression. Our initial concern then is not to find a solution; *our initial concern is to realize that there is a problem which needs a solution.* This is the first step—AWARENESS.

SELF-DIAGNOSIS

Next, our awareness must expand to comprehend just what our problem really is. We must diagnose ourselves and the diagnosis must be accurate if the SOUL SURGERY is to be successful. A doctor who diagnoses an upset stomach when the problem is a burst appendix will certainly not be able to help his patient or correct the condition. If we shy away from pinpointing the problem we will never be able to get to the root cause of our predicament.

One of the most prevalent reasons for not being able to pinpoint our trouble is our natural tendency to externalize the blame. We like to think that our troubles are caused by someone or something "out there." We say, "I inherited diabetes from my parents," not realizing that as part of a perfect Creator we inherit only health and wholeness and that we are privileged to exercise our free-will to disavow any other inheritance. We think "my husband has given me a terrible inferiority complex," forgetting that we can be offered things but they become ours only when we accept them. We balk at taking the blame for our own limitations and so we tend to gloss over the *real* cause of our present troubles. It's so easy to explain away an uncomfortable matter by placing the blame away from us. "It's not my fault that . . . ," "He made me . . . ," "I can't help it that . . . ," "It's just my luck . . ." We should realize that these kinds of excuses help no one—certainly they do not help us. In fact, excuses do more to harm us because they further impress our sub-conscious with the belief that events "out there" can affect us. And this is a dangerous belief—it is a false belief. It is a belief based on *appearances* instead of *truth*.

The first step is to become aware that we have a problem and then to identify what that problem is. We have to get to the bottom line by asking "Why, why, why?" until we have exhausted all possible answers. It is difficult to completely overcome an unsatisfactory situation without first finding its real cause. A proper diagnosis can be crucial to our success.

INNER AWARENESS

There is an Intelligence in each of us which can respond only when we recognize it. We communicate with this Intelligence through that quality of consciousness which we call *inner awareness*. In order to determine the real cause of our problem it is important that we communicate with this inner awareness. We can do this only by regularly "tuning in" to that still, small voice within us that knows all and seeks to tell us all. We can achieve this communication through regular, daily meditation, by sitting calmly in quiet expectation and listening carefully for the murmurings of our spirit.

THE ULTIMATE CAUSE

In an effort to more fully understand how a problem manifests itself, we should know that involved in any event there are many causes. We will borrow from Aristotle, who identified four causes in every event. We will call them the *external cause*, the *obvious cause*, the *essential cause* and the *ultimate cause*. Every event can be broken down into these four causes.

Take, for example, the automobile you drive. The *external cause* of the automobile is the metal, glass, chrome, rubber, plastic and paint which make it up. The *obvious cause* is the tire makers, painters and autoworkers who put it together. The essential cause is the design or blueprint of the car that the workers follow to build it. But the *ultimate cause* is the need for transportation.

In the case of a raincoat the external cause is the material it is made of. The obvious cause is the tailor who made it. The essential cause is the pattern that the tailor followed. The ultimate cause, however, is the need for protection.

An overweight woman's problem can be analyzed in much the same way. The external cause is too much fat; the obvious cause is her eating too much or exercising too little; the essential cause could be her poor self-image; but the ultimate cause might be her need for an excuse to be less popular than a beautiful older sister or the need to be like the rest of the family who are all overweight, or a hundred other reasons for which the soul has need.

When we have identified our situation and broken it down into these four categories we can more easily work towards a solution because we will have identified the root cause.

The external cause and the obvious cause are really superficial causes and can only be dealt with superficially. They are the purview of the medical doctor, the marriage counselor, the psychiatrist and the minister. We can never totally solve our problems by dealing *only* at these levels.

Let's take, for example, a bad cold that puts us in bed for a few days. The external cause of the cold is the sneezing, running nose, fever, etc. The obvious cause is our getting caught in the rain the day before or someone's sneezing on us in the elevator or sleeping next to our mate who has a cold, or numerous other reasons. These causes are in the physical world and thus in the realm of medical science. We can take cold medication, we can stay in bed and keep warm, we can avoid contact with those who have colds. But these remedies in themselves will not prohibit our getting other colds because we have not dealt with the deeper causes—the essential cause and the ultimate cause—which are lodged in our mind, in our soul.

The essential cause of the cold is our *belief* that "this is the cold season" or "the flu is going around" or "keep buttoned up or you'll catch a cold." We can choose to believe that a change in season can bring a change in our health. Or we can choose to believe that sickness floats around waiting to pounce on the unwary. Or we can believe that we can "catch" a cold or, more to the point, that a cold can "catch" us! We lay the foundation of our sickness by our persistent thoughts and beliefs. If our persistent thoughts and beliefs are of sickness and worry and fear of sickness, then a foundation of ill-health will be firmly rooted in our mind, in our soul.

Finally, the ultimate cause of our sickness is our need for pity, or our desire to skip a day of work, or our need to stay home and avoid an unpleasant situation or any of a plethora of needs which a cold will fulfill. We very often choose to get sick when we feel we have nothing better to do. Or, it could be that a suitable sickness will give us something that we feel we can't get in any other way, like sympathy or a demonstration of affection from someone.

WORK IS DONE WITHIN

The essential cause and the ultimate cause are areas which only we can change. There is no medication or exercise or change in climate which can do it for us. It is work which must be done within. It must be done by purging the false beliefs which have attached themselves so tenaciously to our soul.

As already mentioned, the best way for us to become aware of these erroneous beliefs and crippling needs is to engage in regular, quiet meditation. There is no area of human endeavor which can pay as great a dividend as regular meditation. Meditation allows us to get in touch with that unchanging aspect of us. This quiet time allows us to contact that Intelligence deep within us which will always tell us (if we will only slow down enough to listen) what to do. Regular meditation is the quickest and surest way to increase our awareness and should become an important part of our daily activity.

PROBLEMS SERVE OUR PURPOSE

We are sick or poor or lonely because sickness, poverty, or loneliness is serving the purpose of our soul. If we want to remove these bitter fruits from our lives, we must stop seeking nourishment from the depleted soil of appearances. We must uproot all false beliefs and replant our thoughts in the rich compost of God's love, for *only when our roots reach deeply into the Truth of our being can our lives bear the rich fruit of God's abundance.*

HEADING HOME

Our first step then is one of AWARENESS. We must become aware that we have a problem and also become aware of just what that problem is doing to us. Then we should pinpoint what that problem really is. Just as we will not find the proper direction to take us home until we first realize that we are lost and then pinpoint our location on a map, so we can never find the direction to our "true home" unless we take the same steps. We must realize that we are traveling away from our good and next find out why.

If we have seriously searched our soul and can not find the elusive ultimate cause of our present difficulty, we should not give up. We should go on to the next step aware, at least, that a problem does exist and that we will eventually isolate it and excise it from our soul.

The Jews of the Old Testament wandered in the desert, unaware that the promised land lay so close by but aware at least that they were lost. And so they persisted in searching for their home and the good that awaited them there. Finally, after forty years, they found it. However, had they not taken that crucial first step—had they not been *aware* that they were lost—they would never have continued in their search.

Awareness is the beginning of the end of our wanderings. Once we are conscious of being lost we will have taken the first step toward our promised land and the good that awaits us there. We, too, will be going home!

Chapter V

BLESSING

When we bless a problem it soon blesses us.

The second step in our SOUL SURGERY is BLESSING. Every situation with which we are confronted, whether it be in our body or in our outer affairs—*every situation*—contains somewhere within it the seed of our good. It does not matter how negative it may appear to us, to our friends, to our doctor, to our lawyer, to our psychiatrist, to our marriage counselor or to anyone. Jesus admonished us to "Judge not according to appearances but judge righteous judgment." In other words, we must not draw any conclusions from how things *seem to be*. We can only interpret "appearances" by the use of our five senses and, as we have seen, our senses are very fallable instruments with which to judge our entire existence.

All "victories" and "defeats" begin in man's mind. This is a crucial concept. What it means is that whatever has happened in our outer world has had its *beginnings* in our mind—in our thoughts and ideas. The unfoldment of that thought was simply an example of the law of mind action, which is, "thoughts held in mind produce after their kind." Those thoughts which we accept as being true and then dwell on will eventually manifest in our lives and affairs. In other words, if we dwell on thoughts of sickness then we can never expect abundant health in our lives. If we dwell on thoughts of poverty we can never expect prosperity in our lives. If we dwell on thoughts of hatred then we can never have love in our lives. Such thoughts of sickness and poverty and hatred, along with thoughts such as fear and lack and many others, are thoughts which are not based on Truth but are based instead on appearances.

It so often seems that events in our lives have a power of their own—a power to overwhelm us. But, in truth, they don't. In truth the circumstances we fear are not all-powerful but are actually subject to our thoughts about them.

Therefore, we must learn to forget about how things look. We should not make a decision about a situation based only on how it *appears* to us. Instead ". . . judge righteous judgment." Know that the universe is always good and that good is in *every* situation.

When we "judge righteous judgment," when we know that God is present in every event in our lives, then we can bless the event, knowing that our good will soon be manifest. As soon as we proclaim good then good becomes our world. As soon as we bless a problem then that problem soon blesses us.

WE DETERMINE OUR GOOD

It is we who have the power to change any situation by merely declaring it "good" or "evil." When we accept an event as negative or evil we attach that evil to us more firmly. We embrace it and having embraced it we give it dominion over us. We allow it to block the flow of goodness through us. The false belief roots itself in our soul and grows larger and more important in our lives by feeding on our own fears and self-pity. The false belief which we have embraced now begins to embrace us, strangling us with its growth. Its roots begin reaching into all aspects of our lives, retarding the clear flow of Truth from spirit and suffocating our good.

However, when we bless a situation and decree it good we open our minds to the streaming abundance of all of God's gifts. We become masters of our world and the powers of the universe are ours. The elements over which we have been given dominion become responsive to us and the good that we have pictured in our minds soon manifests in our lives.

YOU ARE NOT ALONE

When we alter our perception, our thoughts and our consciousness, we don't have to alter our situation! When we bless and keep blessing what seems to be a negative situation we accomplish two things. First of all we come to realize that we are not "fighting the battle" alone. Whatever negative-seeming event has appeared, if we bless it and pronounce it good we know that God is there and that we are not facing it by ourselves; we know that the power of the universe is behind us! This is a great comfort, for alone we can do nothing, but with God we can do all things.

Secondly, when we bless a situation we untangle ourselves from it. It immediately ceases to be a multi-armed octopus constricting our full expression. We no longer have to struggle and strain, trying to keep the bad out of our lives. Instead we can swim along with the tide, observing events unfold, aware that as long as we keep centered our good is forthcoming.

Let's stop thinking of negative-seeming events as problems or as obstacles. Let's begin treating them instead as "challenges," as situations which provide us with the opportunity to grow.

A body-builder does not resent the heavy weights he must lift in the gym. He does not think of them as "problems" or as "obstacles" which are inhibiting his good. On the contrary, he knows that without the resistance of those heavy weights his muscles would never grow. It is only by meeting the resistance they offer and by overcoming it that his body will assume the proportions that he desires. The heavy weights are a means to his good. Without their resistance he could never accomplish his goal. A body-builder does not curse the weights for suppressing his good. He blesses them for giving him a chance to grow.

And we should do the same. Loneliness, poverty, sickness—these are among the challenges, these are the resistances, which force us to grow. And we should bless them because we can only grow to the extent of the resistance offered. We stop ascending the mountain when we run out of mountain to climb. As long as there is a problem in our lives we know we have a weakness, a deficiency, an area which needs attention. We bless this problem because it points out to us an opportunity for more growth.

FORGIVE YOUR ENEMY

Almost invariably the need for a healing in our body or affairs is linked with an unwillingness to love or forgive.

That is why our greatest "teachers" are those people whom we hate or dislike or who stand in opposition to us, for they give us a chance to see our weakness.

Since all things and all persons are merely reflections of us, we should bless and keep on blessing those very persons whom we have trouble loving. A mirror reflects back to us precisely where our face is dirty but we don't hate the mirror! No, we are thankful for having something which shows us where we need help. And that is precisely why we must bless our "enemies." Like a mirror, our "enemies" can teach us the most about ourselves because they unerringly reflect back to us our limitations.

If we truly desire a healing, we must first overcome all of our hates or dislikes because it is that very feeling which is the limiting factor in the healing of our body and bodily affairs. Hatred is a prison which confines those who hate. The only way to escape this prison is to love your way out! Healing follows forgiveness and the forgiveness must be complete and unequivocal. Often, when we feel we are forgiving we are merely rearranging our prejudices. If we feel the other person "won't listen" or refuses to see "our side," this is not forgiveness! This is an attempt at justification and justification of one's own viewpoint is not forgiveness. Forgiveness transcends finding blame. It transmits a message of love from Christ-center to Christ-center and wipes the slate clean.

SELF-PITY STOPS GROWTH

We grow most steadily when we bless and love someone who doesn't love us. And we regress most surely when our self-pity makes us keep right on hating. If there is an enemy of growth and self-unfoldment in our lives it is self-pity because self-pity causes us to back away from hurt and disappointment and not face it down. We are coming face-to-face with a limitation in ourself and we are not able to cope with it! Instead of acting from our Christ-consciousness and blessing the person or event, we act from our sense consciousness and withdraw into a defensive shell of self-pity. Even the timid turtle must first stick out his head from his defensive shell of safety if he is ever to move forward. And we too must eventually move out of our defensive shell of self-pity if we are ever to move forward in consciousness.

BLESSING RELEASES US

There are many times when we are afraid to bless any situation we hate because we think that this will attach us more firmly to it, but quite the opposite is true. We must love ourselves out of every situation. We must bless our limitations. In doing so we are not drawing them closer. In blessing them we have admitted to ourselves that there is an area in our lives which needs attention and that the person or event involved has shown us what it is. The event then is *detached* from our lives. In accepting the situation it remains a problem but in blessing it we change it from a problem to an opportunity.

Another benefit we accrue from blessing our enemies or our present predicament is that it gives us a chance to begin ridding ourselves of all past accumulations of hate which cling to our soul like so many parasites. In blessing our lives and in affirming our good for ourselves we weaken their grip on us. The more we bless them the weaker they get. When we act from our Christ-center, when we send out the warm rays of love that are in us, people sense this, they do not feel challenged and their defenses drop. Then they begin treating us as we treat them.

SEEING OURSELVES IN OTHERS

People's responses to us *always* exactly correspond to our most deeply held feelings about them. What we see in them are our own concepts reflected back to us. As we see others, so we are seen by them. When we look at others we are actually seeing ourselves. The faults we find exist in us. The beauty we find exists in us. To change the outward impression we must first change the inner thought. What we want to *see* on our "outside" we must first *become* on our "inside."

Our bodies and outer affairs are mirror reflections of the state of our soul. We have only to look at the state of our outer world to see what our most intimately held beliefs are. And because of that fact we should rejoice at our challenge because it is the superficial manifestation of a more deeply hidden malignancy. If our neighbor hates us, then this is an indication to us that we must expand *our* love consciousness. If our boss refuses to give us a raise, then this is an indication to us that we must expand *our* prosperity consciousness. If we are constantly concerned for the well-being of a loved one, then this is an indication to us that we must expand *our* faith consciousness. We cannot see our souls, that is true, but we can see the mirror reflections of our souls—our bodies and outer affairs— and we can use these reflections to examine our souls more closely.

THE POWER OF PRONOUNCING JUDGMENT

In the classic fairy tale, "The Beauty and the Beast," a young maiden is taken captive by a horrible looking beast and is held by him against her will. The beast is enamored by the fair maiden and asks her to marry him. She is repulsed by the beast and vehemently refuses. He follows her around day after day, persisting in his proposals and she just as persistently declines. She pines away for her freedom and eventually despairs of ever ridding her life of the repugnant beast. Finally, feeling compassion for the creature, she does consent to marry him. Upon agreeing to do so, he is immediately transformed into a handsome prince who takes her to his splendid kingdom where they live happily ever after.

Like the maiden, we must realize that what may appear "ugly" to us on the outside will harbor our good if we will only bless it. The maiden blessed the beast. Her consent to marry it was really a commitment to love it—to bless it—and that very act pronounced the situation good. Within the seemingly horrible predicament in which she found herself was the seed of her happiness "ever after." In finally acting from her Christ-center she changed the negative situation into a positive one.

The "beasts" in our lives are the false beliefs and the negative appearances which keep us captive. We can never escape their powerful grip until we realize that within each predicament are sown the seeds of our salvation. We can only "live happily ever after" when we bless the situation and allow our good to be released out of it.

Let us never forget that our ability to bless a painful predicament in our lives is one of the greatest assets that we possess. This power of pronouncing judgment can transform the situation and transform us. It can transport us to new spiritual, mental and physical plateaux or it can plunge us into the depths of loneliness, poverty, hatred and sickness.

If there is a persistent problem in your life which has been following you around, don't run away from it any longer. Stop, turn around and confront the trouble face-to-face, knowing that within even the most negative appearance exists the seed of your good. Bless that problem and claim your good now.

Chapter VI

COMMITMENT

No great deeds are ever completed without great commitments.

Commitment is the necessary third step in our SOUL SURGERY. We have to *want* to change our lives before we will ever take the first steps to do so. A sincere and genuine desire will lead to a sincere and genuine commitment. The firmer our desire, the firmer will be our commitment. If we have a strong desire to overcome a problem, then the strength of our commitment will perfectly reflect this desire. And it is ultimately the strength of our commitment which is the motivation for our actions. We will do something about our problem only to the extent that our commitment motivates us to do so. As soon as our motivation ceases our actions cease.

No great deeds are ever completed without great commitments to those deeds, for commitment is basic to any meaningful change. But every problem presents us with two choices in treating it. Two separate voices vie for our attention and the choice we make is critical to our ultimate unfoldment. When trouble develops and a seemingly insurmountable problem faces us we can listen to that still small voice deep within us which looks to the truth of the situation and gently urges us to face the challenge, commit ourselves to overcoming it and dare to take action. Or, we can tune in to the noisy ramblings of our senses, which look only at outer appearances and tell us "the problem can't be solved," or "don't rock the boat," or "don't worry about it, you can always do it later." The voice that we listen to and the extent to which we obey it will determine the effect of the problem on us. If we listen to the inharmony of sense impressions we will soon be convinced of the invincibility of the problem and of our helplessness in the face of such "bad luck."

If, on the other hand, we heed that core of Truth within us which tells us that our desire to change our life is really a perfect universe prodding us to express more and more of *our* perfection, then the "insurmountable" problem will shrink to the insignificance of mere appearance and will eventually become a stepping stone to our good.

Choose Your Partner

The choice is ours. We can become like a whirling dervish, gyrating feverishly to the frenzied tempo of appearances which our five limited senses interpret and orchestrate daily. Or we can waltz gracefully to the soothing, pulsating rhythm of a universe which proclaims our immunity from anything but our good. The voice that we heed will mold our commitment and will eventually produce a corresponding manifestation in our lives and affairs.

Unless we are strongly committed to overcoming our problem—to improving our lives—we run the risk of giving up before we have reached our final goal. The faculty of zeal is essential. Without it we are like a powerful engine with too little fuel—rich in potential but poor in effectiveness. But even zeal is worthless unless we know what it is we want to do!

CLARIFY YOUR GOAL

If our desire is left undirected it will soon dissipate into the ephemeral world of wishful thinking. No matter how fervent our desire to accomplish something, no matter how zealously we want to pursue it, if we leave it in the form of a vague longing we will never be able to harness it into the motivation that will drive us toward our good. For example, we may want to "get away from it all" for a few weeks and go on a vacation. But if, when we are asked at the airplane ticket counter where we want to go and we answer "I'm not quite sure" or "I don't really know," then we will never go anyplace! Our desire must never be allowed to become merely half-hearted hoping or wishful thinking.

We can never reach a goal that does not exist! It is not enough just to want to be successful. In what area do you want to be successful? Do you want to be a successful writer, a successful salesman, a successful executive, a successful mother, a successful entrepreneur? The desire is clear—success—but the goal has not yet been brought into focus and is, therefore, unreachable.

USE YOUR IMAGINATION

So, before we can make a meaningful commitment, we must first have a firm goal in mind. Not only must it be firm, it must also be rational and reachable. A frail, five foot tall women may want to play professional football, but is her goal rational and reachable? Can she *really* believe that she can compete with six foot six inch, two hundred fifty pound men? The *meaningful* goals in our life *are* attainable. *Anything* which is true of us in God's realm is rational and reachable. In God's realm we are perfectly whole and healthy, therefore, perfect health is a rational and reachable goal. In God's realm we are filled with love, therefore, to be loved is a rational and reachable goal. In God's realm we share all of His abundance, therefore, prosperity is a rational and reachable goal. Any of the perfect attributes which we share with God as individualized expressions of Him are rational and reachable goals and we can express them in our bodies and affairs.

If we cannot envision our ultimate success, however, then all of our efforts are doomed before we even begin. We can and should use the most creative of our mind powers—imagination—to help us in this area. There is no mind power more creative than the power to envision, to imagine. By consciously directing our minds to hold a definite, firmly pictured goal, we will subconsciously direct our lives toward the attainment of that goal. Imagination can awaken within us our inner forces. It can stir into action those latent powers which otherwise would never come to the surface because imagination carries with it those feelings and emotions which prod us into action. One thing we can be sure of, when we mentally "see" our good—although we still don't physically possess it—the law of mind action will work toward the fulfillment of that good. Of course we must put forth effort, but if we are able to *see* our good as already manifested it is easier to work toward that good.

Consider a man walking in the desert—lost, tired and badly in need of water. As long as there appear before him only sand dunes, it is very difficult for him to be motivated to keep on walking. He is aware of the heat, his thirst, his burning feet, his weary body. But let him stand atop a dune and see an oasis in the distance and his motivation is immediately renewed. Suddenly the heat, the thirst and the weariness disappear from his mind. His commitment is now single-minded. Now he can *see* his goal and all of his effort will be directed toward attaining it.

If we are "thirsting" for deliverance from a problem, it behooves us to "see" our goal clearly and distinctly. It benefits us to get a definite goal in mind and keep it in mind. Every time we think of ourselves we will image ourselves as having attained our goal. We will think of ourselves exactly the way we want to be and this will give us the impetus to attain it. *We cannot help becoming that which we believe ourselves to be.*

MAKE A COVENANT

Our desire must be forged into a solid commitment and this commitment must be impressed upon our subconscious by our daily thoughts, words and deeds.

One of the most effective ways to show our commitment is to write out in the form of a covenant exactly what we want to accomplish. This is an important tool at our disposal and one that will help to solidify our desire.

There is no one format which would serve all covenants. Our covenant is between us and God and it is important that it be motivating and meaningful to us. In order to be most effective, however, there are certain things a covenant should contain.

Every covenant should begin with an acknowledgement of God as the ultimate Source of our good. This is a basic truth which we often need to be reminded of. The realization that with God we can do all things is the very crux of our deliverance from any negative situation.

Stating our goal should be the next step. Just exactly what are we trying to accomplish? We should be specific and realistic and also be sure our goal is for the good of *all* concerned. To the extent that our goal is for the good of all, to that extent we will succeed in attaining it.

Next we list each step we will take in working with God to accomplish our goal. We promise to take them, knowing that God can only help us when He can work *with* us. His strength can only supplement *our* effort. What will *we* do about attaining our goal? What actions will *we* take to change our situation? A well thought-out plan of action is written so that we have a definite strategy to follow.

The covenant is a "contract" between us and God. We end it by expressing thanks and showing faith that as long as we honor our promises we know that God will honor His and that our desire will be fulfilled.

After carefully wording our convenant to include all of these things, we should sign it, date it and post it in a conspicuous place where we will see it daily. In this way, having pledged our desire for change, we will have impressed our subconscious mind with the sincerity of our undertaking. A covenant is a pledge, an avowal. When we take the time to write out a convenant and sign it we will not take lightly the promise it contains.

Verbalizing our commitment as a covenant helps us to more sharply focus on and clarify our main goal. It allows us to concentrate our attention and our resources more fully on our primary objective rather than scatter our attention on some ill-defined hopes.

It becomes a daily reminder which keeps us on a single track and restrains our straying from the desired path. Success, after all, comes from single-mindedness, from not allowing our mind to be swayed by outside conditions, not allowing it to be cluttered with fear of failure, discouragement, lack of faith and forebodings of calamity.

A well thought-out covenant will help us to keep from contradicting by our actions the commitment that we have made in our heart. The law of cause and effect, we must remember, is activated by our thoughts and by the deep desires of our heart. When we verbalize in the form of a covenant those thoughts and deep desires, we also unleash the powerful law of mind action which is that "thoughts held in mind produce after their kind." In other words, that which dominates our thinking, that which our mind dwells on, will ultimately be the thing which manifests in our lives. If we dwell on failure then failure will be our lot. If we dwell on calamity then calamity will be our lot. *A covenant forces us to dwell on success.* It leaves no room for nor does it consider failure as a viable alternative. *Success, therefore, becomes our lot.*

AN IMPORTANT STEP

A firm commitment, then, is an important step in our SOUL SURGERY. We must spend a good deal of time determining just what our goal is—just what we are trying to accomplish. We should write out and sign a covenant. It will help our focus and our motivation and the very composing of it will help us to better clarify the challenge that we face and the means we must take to uncover our good.

Remember, great deeds need great commitments to those deeds. We will never express the greatness and the splendor which is within us until we commit ourselves to doing so. If our commitment is shallow our actions will be limited. If our actions are limited our results will be incomplete. The height of our success will mirror the breadth of our actions but the breadth of our actions can only reflect the depth of our commitment.

Chapter VII

DENIALS AND AFFIRMATIONS

Like spiritual training wheels, denials and affirmations assist us as we seek to find our divine equilibrium.

The next step in our quest for perfection is to DENY what is false about our problem and to AFFIRM the Truth of the situation. In chapter five we learned that the seed of our good lies in *every* problem and in *every* challenge which faces us. No matter what the appearance, we hold fast to the knowledge that our good is imminent. We do not judge by appearances but instead we "judge righteous judgment." In using righteous judgment we measure all situations by applying the principles of Truth and not the pronouncement of appearances. In doing so we are relying on spiritual realities and not sense impressions. The limited reports of the five senses can never accurately convey the whole truth of any situation.

THERE IS ONLY GOOD

Deep in our heart of hearts, in our holy of holies, in the perfect center of each of us resides an assurance that "there is one Presence and one Power in my life, God the good omnipotent.'' Every student of Truth instinctively knows this. The Universal Life Force which created all is present in all Its creations; It powers all of Its creations and It works for the good of all of Its creations. Why would It do otherwise? How can there be any questioning of this? This is the Truth we must always hold to when challenged by a seemingly insurmountable trouble—''There is one Presence and one Power in my life: God, the good omnipotent. And since God is the only Presence then He must be present in this situation. Therefore I have only to act from my perfect center and all will work for my good.''

Let's face the fact that it is *we* who make all appearances. We name something ''good'' and another thing ''evil'' according to our impression of it. God furnishes us with the raw material and this is *always* good. We cannot pollute God's gifts but we can see them ''through a glass darkly'' and *think* they're polluted.

All in our lives is of good because all is of God. This is the consciousness from which we must always act.

SPIRITUAL AMNESIA

We run into trouble when, for one reason or another, we fall into a state of spiritual amnesia and forget our true relationship with our good. We name one situation ''good'' and another one ''evil,'' and by that very declaration allow that situation to affect our lives. When we declare a situation ''good'' and hold good in our mind then our good is inevitable. Conversely, when we declare a situation ''evil'' and hold that thought in our mind then we are affected in a negative way. ''Thoughts held in mind produce after their kind.'' Is it not a logical progression to see that good thoughts eventually produce good manifestations and evil or bad thoughts produce bad manifestations?

CONSCIOUSNESS CULTIVATORS

It is our consciousness then which must be brought into line with the Truth of our being. And that is why the use of denials and affirmations can be so important to our success. Denials and affirmations are "consciousness cultivators." In the fertile garden of our mind we use denials to pull the weeds of sense consciousness and affirmations to plant the flowers of spiritual consciousness. They can realign our thinking along the lines of Truth. Like spiritual training wheels, denials and affirmations assist us as we seek to find our divine equilibrium.

Since "like attracts like" we want our thoughts to be of good so that we will attract good to us. This is not to say that we can use denials and affirmations to manipulate someone else's consciousness or to manipulate outer reality, for *we can only deny that which is false and affirm that which is true* and that is all we should ever deny or affirm.

When we state, for example, "Pain and sickness are not real and cannot affect me," we are not implying that we have never felt pain or sickness or any other negative condition. What we are stating is that these conditions do not have a reality, a power or a dominion of their own and therefore cannot have a reality, power or dominion in our lives unless we allow them to do so. That unnatural tissue mass appearing on the X-ray of a man's lungs cannot be denied, it clearly shows on the film. But he can deny the *inevitability* of this tissue mass to remain in his body. He can deny the *power* of this tissue mass to affect him any longer. When he denies this "dis-ease" any dominion or power over him, he cuts out its root system and robs it of all nourishment. Without nourishment the tissue mass will waste away until it completely disappears from his life. The "reality" of the disease, therefore, was not in his lungs but in his mind. When we repeat a denial we are not denying the appearances of a situation, *we are merely denying the reality of those appearances and denying them any power over us.*

WORK ONLY WITH TRUTH

Both denials and affirmations must always be rooted in Truth. Something is not false just because we deny it; rather, *we deny it because it is false.* Conversely, something is not true just because we affirm it; *we affirm it because it is true.* This is an important distinction.

We can never deny something out of existence nor can we ever affirm something into existence. We can, however, deny our inaccurate thoughts and feelings about something and affirm those thoughts and feelings based on Truth. When we do this we change our consciousness and our changed consciousness eventually draws to us our good.

"Prayer does not change things, prayer changes people and people change things!" Thoughts produce according to their character. When we align our thoughts with the Truth of our being, we produce good in our lives. By using denials to repudiate a negative condition based on appearances and then using affirmations to ratify a positive principle based on Truth, we change our consciousness in such a way that good becomes our world.

DENIALS

Isn't it marvelous that we, along with all other forms of life on this planet, have been given the power of elimination! Without elimination we would have no way to rid our bodies of the toxic wastes of metabolism. We would have no way of excluding those life-denying poisons which accumulate daily as a result of normal living. But the fact is that we are able through our intestines, kidneys, skin and lungs to excrete these metabolic wastes. In doing so—in denying these life-depleting poisons a place in our body—we strengthen those life-sustaining forces which keep us whole and healthy.

However, the faculty of elimination is not the exclusive purview of our physical bodies. We have been given the ability to eliminate or deny anything in our life which is not sustaining and nurturing our good. When we deny, we use our power of elimination—we say NO to all that is contrary to truth.

Denial is a tool which can be used to remove from our consciousness all beliefs that are not consistent with the highest expression of the Truth of our being. Denial is the highest form of judgment, for in denying we refuse to accept a limiting belief as being true. We purge from our lives that which is keeping us from expressing our perfect-selves. It is important to again note that we do not deny anything out of existence, we merely deny our incorrect beliefs about it. For instance, a man manifesting alcoholism cannot deny his excess consumption of alcohol—he cannot dismiss such an obvious fact. He may not even be able to deny his desire for alcohol. However, he can deny being in bondage to alcohol, he can deny being controlled by it. Having denied the thought that he "can't resist" alcohol and that alcohol "has dominion" over him, he is on his way toward overcoming alcoholism. He has not denied the fact that he drinks alcohol nor that he often craves it but he has denied the *inevitability* of having to drink it. In denying this inevitability, he has opened up his consciousness to accepting the fact that alcohol is not an inevitable part of his life unless *he* allows it to be so. As this consciousness expands he soon sees that he has been given dominion over *all* things—not only alcohol—and that he is in bondage to nothing. Alcohol then becomes unimportant in his life because it is a drug—a poison—and it will pollute his sacred body temple. He simply does not need alcohol, therefore he does not use it.

Any true denial is not concerned with things or conditions; it is concerned with our incorrect beliefs which bring about the unsavory conditions. When denials are properly utilized the unsavory predicament disappears because the *error in consciousness which produced it is erased.* Thoughts produce according to their character. Denials remove the distorted, self-defeating concepts which distort our lives. We are the result of all that we have believed but our list of beliefs contains an abundance of incorrect assumptions. These old mental structures must be razed to the ground. We must "die daily." We can only fear when we believe in an evil. Deny the evil and lose the fear.

In chapter four we learned that the first step in SOUL SURGERY is to become AWARE of the reason for our problem—to admit to ourselves the cause. Having admitted the error we must now deny its power so that our consciousness can be purged of its false belief.

Make Them Meaningful To You

Denials are most effective when structured in a simple sentence and said aloud as often as possible. Although it is always the ideas behind the denial statement which give impetus to our change of consciousness, the actual words can be a great motivator in helping us. For instance, one manifesting alcoholism may try to convince his intellect by saying, "I will not drink alcohol because I don't like it."

But this denial may be untrue and he would have a difficult time convincing himself. It might be more effective for him to say, "I will not drink alcohol because I don't *need* it," to "I am created perfect and am not in bondage to anything." His intellect can completely agree with those statements and so it is easier for him to incorporate them into his consciousness.

THE POSITIVE POWER OF NO

Some persons don't like to use denials; they think of them as "too negative" and choose to use only affirmations instead. But using affirmations without denials is like changing a baby's diaper by putting a clean one over a soiled one! And denials, when used properly, are *not* negative. The proper use of denials is the use of the POSITIVE power of "no."

Before any rebuilding can take place in our lives or affairs, we must first remove whatever it is which is causing us trouble. If our house were on fire, wouldn't we first call a fireman *before* calling a building contractor to rebuild it? If there were a disease organism in our body, wouldn't we first see that it was removed *before* choosing a diet and exercise to rebuild our body? In much the same way, denials allow us to first remove what is wrong in our lives— our wrong beliefs—*before* we begin rebuilding our consciousness.

Since what we believe in we serve and are served by, *as we change our wrong beliefs we change our body and affairs.* Denials are an important step in this change. Just as a body can't be perfect with a disease organism in it, we can't be perfect if we haven't first eliminated the "diseased" thoughts of hatred, sickness, poverty and other such corrupt beliefs from our minds. How can we fill our lives with love if we haven't first removed the disease thought of hatred? How can we fill our lives with health if we haven't first removed the disease thought of sickness? How can we fill our lives with prosperity if we haven't first removed the disease thought of poverty? We can't plant a flower on top of a weed!

MEAN WHAT YOU SAY

Each thought of sickness or health, hatred or love, poverty or prosperity cuts a very subtle "groove" in the brain, strengthening the tendency toward whatever thought is dominant. Therefore, in order to be whole and healthy, our positive thoughts of health, love and prosperity must be impregnated with such will power that they will resist any contrary thoughts. Whatever thoughts are most dominant will cut the deepest "grooves."

Repeat your denials as often as possible. It is not necessary that they be said aloud, although when this is possible it should be done. And whenever they are said, either silently or audibly, they should be said with *conviction*. A thought without conviction behind it has no value. But when your words are saturated with faith, sincerity and conviction—when they are potent with soul vibration— they are like powerful explosives which will shatter the old rocks of negative beliefs, clearing the way for the growth of a new, higher state of consciousness.

If we are faithful in our denials of negative thoughts or untrue beliefs, they will be erased and excluded from our consciousness and the unpleasant conditions which were produced by that consciousness will change to mirror the new mental pictures presented by affirmations.

AFFIRMATIONS

DYING TO THE OLD IS NOT ENOUGH

In an attempt to improve their downtown area, the city council of a large northeastern city decided to tear down their decrepit and dangerous slum areas. They razed the abandoned buildings, burned-out homes and tenements. However, they found that the areas eventually became as seedy and as undesirable as before as the old slums were slowly replaced by new ones. The city council then realized that it was not enough merely to remove the offending structures. They had to replace them with attractive, functional structures such as theater complexes, shopping malls and apartment houses. After this was done, the slums did not return.

This "born again" city offers a great lesson for us. If we are to be born again in consciousness we must die to the old "decrepit and dangerous" beliefs that we have been harboring. But when we clear this error consciousness from our minds we must then remember to follow it with the establishment of a Truth consciousness or else the error thinking will filter back and we will have to dislodge it again and again.

AFFIRMATIONS ESTABLISH TRUTH CONSCIOUSNESS

It is not enough to simply pull the weeds in our garden; we must eventually plant an abundance of flowers so that the weeds wil have nowhere to grow. Denials remove error states of consciousness but they must be followed by affirmations if we are to be completely successful. Affirmations build into that area which was cleansed only those things which are the highest expression of the Truth of our being. Affirmations take an idea from Divine Mind, which we have special need of at that moment, and root it deeply in the soil of our consciousness.

An affirmation is a tool which establishes in our mind the truth about a situation based on the omnipresence of God. Its primary purpose is to build a consciousness of the presence of God (and therefore our good) in every event in our lives. We use affirmations to convince the intellect and the emotions of the truth of the matter—that God is the only presence and power in the universe.

Like denials, affirmations should be repeated, either silently or audibly, as often as possible. In doing so it is important that we remind ourselves that our affirmations are not "making something come into existence." What we are doing when we affirm is to claim the good that is ours by divine inheritance and secure the expectation of that good in our consciousness. Affirmations help us to see clearly that which we are capable of becoming.

The constant repetition of an affirmation is important because this imbeds the idea behind the affirmation deeply in our subconscious mind or feeling nature. When the subconscious and the conscious mind (feeling and thinking) agree, the idea becomes part of our consciousness, "plugging into" the law that assures its fulfilling. When we speak our affirmations with faith, joy and enthusiasm we hasten the fulfilling of our good. "What things soever ye desire, when ye pray, believe that ye receive them, and ye shall have them."

MIND CONDITIONS BODY

Affirmations do not work only in the realm of nebulous spiritual and mental laws. Our human bodies are extremely receptive to the bidding of our mind. Any message that we repeat goes through our brain cortex—our frontal lobes and our limbic system, which have to do with our emotions. Deep within this area is the hypothalamus which is the master regulator of the autonomic nervous system and supervisor of many body functions such as pulse rate, blood pressure, hormone production, and body temperature. When we repeat affirmations we are actually conditioning our bodies to do those things which we are affirming. Thus the need for positive affirmations becomes obvious.

THE IMPORTANCE OF "I AM"

Every time we think, we move energy. It is up to us if we move it in a negative way or in a positive way. "Thou shalt also decree a thing and it shall be established unto thee." How can we decree pain, sickness, hatred and poverty and expect health, wholeness, love and prosperity? Our affirmations must not be scattered about aimlessly. And we are guilty of doing this if we follow the words "I am" with statements which are untrue of our real selves. It is important to know that the words "I am" are our individual identification. When we say "I am" we are, in effect, saying "My essence is" or "the truth of my being is." Imagine how our subconscious is affected when we say "*I am* sick," or "*I am* poor," or "*I am* unloved." What our subconscious gleans from this is that "my essence is sickness" or "my essence is poverty," or "my essence is to be unloved!" When we say "I am _____" we are affirming. How can we possibly think that our true nature can be sick or poor or lack love! Instead of saying "I am sick," one should affirm "I am getting better and better each day."

We are constantly building new cells in our bodies—millions every second—and we build them according to our consciousness! How much better it is for us to build them in the consciousness of health. We can't demonstrate health if we dissipate this idea of health by denying it in our conversations.

We can only become that which we believe ourselves to be. When we decree something with assurance we establish that idea in our mind and we are bound to it as if with invisible glue.

LOOK FOR THE SILVER LINING

When we affirm we step out on faith to convince ourselves of the truth. There will be times when we will be hard-pressed to find something affirmative in a situation. At times like this we must intellectually design an affirmation which reflects the real truth of the matter as our spirit knows it. Sometimes we will accept things intellectually but not emotionally. At other times the opposite will be true. That aspect of us which doubts must be convinced by the aspect which believes. If we can neither intellectually nor emotionally accept a truth, then we are not ready to change. However, if we truly desire a change, we will be able to discern the truth underlying the problem and will be able to design a suitable denial and affirmation. Once we begin saying them often enough we will experience a healing—but the healing will be of our unbelief! When a truth is repeated enough times it sets up a powerful pattern which overcomes all human fallible reason. It tunes out all static of appearances and tunes in the clear channel of truth. It's not important that we fully believe an affirmation before we begin saying it. The very repetition of it, *if it is true*, will soon convince us of its veracity.

The muscles of a leg which has been in a cast for a long time may be so weakened from lack of use that they are unable to move by themselves. But as a therapist moves the leg and coaxes the muscles to move the muscles soon "remember" their job, slowly gain strength and before long are able to move on their own. The more they are used, of course, the stronger they become.

And so it is with affirmations. We may be just "saying words" with no conviction behind them when we begin. But *if the affirmation is based on Truth* then it will create a momentum of its own and we will finally accept the Truth that it contains.

IMPORTANT TOOLS

DENIALS and AFFIRMATIONS, then, are the fourth step of our SOUL SURGERY. They are tools we can and should use to convince our intellect of the truth in anything which appears negative.

With our superconscious mind we "know." With our conscious mind we "think." And with our subconscious mind we "feel and remember." Denials and affirmations help us to align our thinking, feeling and remembering with that part of us which truly "knows." When we do this, when we mesh the subconscious and conscious into the superconscious, we will have freed our soul of the encumbrances of false beliefs and paved the way for our good to manifest *fully*.

Chapter VIII

EFFORT

A desire without a deed is a dead-end.

There is no more important step in SOUL SURGERY than EFFORT. All steps which have preceded this one are merely techniques to prompt us to take this crucial step. This is not to diminish the importance of the other four; quite the contrary is true. The fact that we are faced with a serious problem in our lives, one which—as was said in the introduction—"overrides all others in significance, one which has persisted in spite of all we have done to overcome it"—means that we have not been able to make an effort or at least the appropriate effort on our own behalf. Most of us can never reach this important step without going through the first four. There can be no *need* of any effort without first an AWARENESS of our problem. There can be no *preparation* for effort without a BLESS-ING of our imminent good which will come out of our problem. There can be no *motivation* to expend effort without a solid COMMITMENT to solving our problem. There can be no *conviction* to our effort without DENIALS and AFFIRMATIONS to remind us of the Truth of our situation.

Need, preparation, motivation and conviction—these are the four prerequisites to any effective and meaningful effort. However, used alone or even together, *they are powerless to change us if we will not act on our own behalf.*

NEED TO FOLLOW THROUGH

What if on the day of a surgical operation the patient were prepared, the operating room were prepared, the surgeon reviewed the operation, changed his clothes, scrubbed up, enthusiastically entered the operating room, looked around and suddenly announced, "Forget the operation, I think I'll play golf today!"

A ridiculous story you say, and you are right. What sane surgeon would ever act in such an irrational way? But can you see a little of yourself in the story? Doesn't it have a counterpart in many of our lives? We recognize an area in our lives which needs attention, we know just what the problem is, we know we should do something about it, we get all excited about changing it and then, when it comes time to act, to do something, to make an effort, we quit and do something easier or more pleasurable?

GOD ANSWERS DEEDS

Perhaps, instead of just completely giving up, we keep praying about the problem, hoping to "pray it away." We entreat God to help us, we plead for assistance, we beg for release. But praying, *by itself*, is not enough. God does not answer our prayers—*God answers our deeds!* Praying to

God does not motivate God into acting on our behalf because *God is always acting on our behalf.* Praying does not change God but it can change us. It can expand our awareness and our consciousness so that *we* will begin acting on our own behalf.

Praying to God to come back into our lives does not bring God back into our lives because *God has never left our lives.* But praying can get *us* to "come back into our lives" and take some action to help ourselves.

Therefore, to pray and beseech God to come to our aid when we will not make an effort on our own behalf is fruitless and unreasonable because God can do for us only what He can do with us. He can do to us only what He can do through us. He has given us all that we need to attain our perfect potential but we *will succeed in reaching our potential only to the extent of the effort we expend on our own behalf.*

Many of us are looking for a healing so that we can continue to live in the same manner as before! The habits that we accumulate during our life are very comfortable. To put forth the effort to break these habits is often more than we are willing to do so we convince ourselves that our problem can be solved by merely affirming our good or by praying for deliverance. But how can we really believe this? It contradicts the Law of Cause and Effect. Yet we are often able to rationalize away the most convincing evidence and so we knowingly break God's laws of health and then expect God to help us when we refuse to make any effort to help ourselves! So we pray to God to cure our ulcer and we keep right on eating hot, spicy foods. We beseech God to strengthen our weak heart but we refuse to exercise. We importune God to make us lose fifty pounds but we continue to reach for second helpings of food. Are these actions rational? God cannot suspend His laws even for a second. Without laws there could be no creation.

GOD IS NOT CAPRICIOUS

What kind of Creator would change His laws at the whim and caprice of His creations? Think of the confusion which would reign in the universe if there were not the solid, dependable Law of Cause and Effect!

Just as the greatest love a parent can show for a child is his allowing the child to leave home and make his own life, so God shows His unlimited love for us by allowing us full freedom to choose our own destiny. And we do this by our obedience or disobedience to the Law.

But the choice is ours. Whenever we make an effort on our own behalf we will automatically reap a benefit to the *exact* extent of our effort. It is the Law! If we want something enough to work for it, we will get it. What could be more fair? The Law of Cause and Effect is the most just concept in the universe. It allows each of us to reap exactly what he sows. It is an iron-clad, gold-plated, diamond-studded guarantee from God that if you seek His kingdom you shall find His kingdom—"seek, and you will find, knock and it will be opened to you." But it is *we* who must do the seeking. It is *we* who must do the knocking. It is *we* who must make the effort.

DESIRE NEEDS A DEED

The crux of the matter is this: *a desire without a deed is a dead end*. No matter how strong our desire, unless we make an effort on our own behalf we cannot and should not expect improvement—it is expecting something for nothing. To believe that some mysterious force is going to enter us and bring us health or love or prosperity after we have willingly disobeyed God's orderly laws, is futile and irrational. How can we believe that we can pray our emphysema away if we keep right on smoking our cigarettes? How can we believe that a certain person will love us if we continue to hate someone else? How can we believe that we can pray money into our pockets if we won't even look for a job? Like a steady wind that *we* must raise our sails to catch, God's strength can only get behind *our* efforts.

AFFIRMATIVE ACTION

We can and should use the techniques of verbal "denials" and "affirmations." These are fine consciousness conditioners. But there is no finer denial than to deny our inaction and no more productive affirmation than affirmative action. We cannot buy our health or our hapiness with our dollars but we can earn our health and happiness with our behavior. Prayers are important—there is no doubt about that, but we must eventually put "feet" on our prayers, for it is only by our striving—by our meeting resistance and overcoming that resistance—that we can grow stronger. A sprinter may train by running long distances with weights attached to his shoes. He welcomes the opportunity to exert a greater effort on his own behalf because he knows that the added resistance will strengthen his legs and increase his speed and stamina. He will grow stronger to the exact extent of the effort he expends.

And so it is with us. We grow by the amount of effort we expend on our own behalf. This is not to say that physical effort is all that can improve us. Some mental and emotional exertions are far more difficult than the most strenuous physical exercise.

For instance, the effort involved in loving someone whom we have formerly hated and whom we feel hates us is purely a mental and spiritual exercise but it may be an extraordinarily difficult thing for us to do. We may have completed all of the other steps of our SOUL SURGERY but our awareness, blessing, commitment, denials and affirmations are useless unless they act as catalysts to get us to make an *effort* to love. Without effort our world will be in the darkness of hatred and resentment and our divinity will stay in a shadowy corner, hidden from our view. But if we make the effort to love, if we try our best to love, then love becomes the great emancipator, freeing us to find our divinity.

IT'S UP TO US

The embryonic chick nestled in the confines of an eggshell has all that it needs within that shell to attain its potential. Nothing can be added—it is a self-contained potential chicken. Similarly we have within us all that we need to attain our potential. We are embryonic divinities and God has placed within us all that we need to attain our divine potential—*nothing* can be added.

As after having made the egg the mother hen can give that embryonic chick only loving warmth to help it hatch, so God, after having made us, can only give us His loving warmth to help us break out of our shell of humanness and realize our full and perfect potential. God determined what we are: divine. But our effort determines what we will become.

ARE YOU WILLING?

We will never be able to unfold all of our perfect potential until we realize that our destiny is in our own hands. We are the surgeons who must operate on our own souls to clear it of all the accumulated debris of error thinking. When we do this, when we act on our own behalf, when we make an effort to find our good, we allow our good to flow through us and our deepest desires become manifest. If we are willing, God is able.

Chapter IX

FAITH

Whatever you ask in prayer, believe that you receive it, and you will.

Mark 11: 24

If our SOUL SURGERY is to be successful—or indeed if we are to even attempt it—there is one faculty of our mind which must be activated after we have become aware of our problem: FAITH. Without at least a modicum of faith in our eventual good we would certainly never dare to BLESS our problem. And it would certainly be foolish to make a COMMITMENT to overcoming the problem if we did not have faith in our ability to do so. The same holds true for repeating DENIALS and AFFIRMATIONS. Why waste time on them—on trying to condition our consciousness—if we have no faith in the eventual outcome? And at least a small amount of faith is necessary if we are to make any meaningful EFFORT on our own behalf! We would never expend an effort on what we thought was a hopeless situation. No one would!

So underlying almost every step of SOUL SURGERY is FAITH. We may not feel any faith when we begin our quest for deliverance from our trouble, but at least a small amount will have to be there none-the-less or else we will give up trying to change our situation and will accept our suffering as inevitable and unchangeable.

Since faith is a necessary prerequisite in getting us to change our lives and our affairs, it is reasonable to assume that if we can expand our faith we will more quickly manifest our good. This expansion of our faith is the object of step six in our SOUL SURGERY.

Faith Says "Yes"

Faith is not so much something to be gained as something we must discover and expand. Faith manifests in our lives on many different levels and in many different ways. However, it finds its most perfect expression in the spiritual nature. Our faith is our highest declaration of our confidence and belief. It is that deep inner assurance that the good we are seeking is already ours.

It is the faculty of faith which allows us to stand surrounded by our problems and affirm our "good" because *faith is the supreme affirmation.* There can be no higher affirmation in our lives than our faith because true faith, in its essence, is an affirmation at the level of spirit. Faith says "yes" to the absolute Truth of our being. It cuts through appearances, it passes beyond hope and trust and belief and firmly roots in the soil of spirit, of knowing.

From Hope to Faith

Although true faith is a power of our spiritual mind, we find faith in various forms in all realms of our existence.

Hope is a very, very distant relative of faith. Hope is not faith but it is usually the first timid step we take on our climb toward faith. The fear or anxiety we feel about our problem will be overcome only when we are able to have our faith in the eventual manifestation of our good. But we are often faced with situations which we feel are so overwhelming that it is almost impossible for us to have faith in this good. However, a part of us will always be able to hope—to wish—and, if that is all we have, then that part should be nurtured so that true faith can eventually bloom.

But hope must go through many transformations before it can become faith. In our journey toward true faith we will pass through "belief" and then "trust." These are parts of our consciousness. They are intellectual choices. Hope and belief and trust are located exclusively in the intellect. They have no contact with spirit. They are intellectual decisions and rely on sense consciousness. But stagnant intellectual faith has within it the seeds of its own destruction because intellect can only "think;" it can never "know." When our faith stops at merely an intellectual faith we are building without substance because when our supporting thoughts change our faith will disappear.

There are no "miracles" possible with intellectual faith alone because by very definition it is limited to what the intellect says is true. And the intellect is limited by impressions from the five senses.

Faith Is a Spiritual Power

True faith, on the other hand, does not rely on sense consciousness. True faith is a spiritual power and is, therefore, always in contact with that unchanging part of us— our spirit. True faith is hope, belief and trust raised from a human consciousness to a cosmic consciousness. Hope, belief and trust is "thinking." Faith is "knowing." Hope, belief and trust are intellectual processes based on reason and logic. Faith is a spiritual process based on eternal Truth. We can have true faith only when we have caught sight of this inner Truth.

When we are spiritually centered our faith is in our imminent good. *Faith is complete confidence in our eventual good.* When we have faith we are building for eternity.

When we anchor our faith at our spiritual center and give ourselves entirely to spirit we are assured that any actions we take are for our good. They *must* be for our good because they were conceived in that part of us which "knows."

SUBSTANCE RESPONDS TO OUR FAITH

Faith is the faculty that carries out the work of affirmations. It is necessary to make affirmations effective. "Like attracts like;" it is the law of mind action. We will attract that which we have faith in. It follows, therefore, that affirming our good *with faith* will bring good into our lives.

Substance responds to our faith in it. Our faith is like a mold which will always be filled with abundance for us. However, the shape of this abundance will be determined by the shape of our faith. We all have the same amount of faith, but each of us invests his faith differently. We can exercise an intellectual faith fed by our sense consciousness and therefore based on appearances, or we can exercise a spiritual faith nurtured by our spiritual consciousness and therefore based on Truth. Our faith can be invested in sickness or it can be invested in health, it can be invested in hatred or it can be invested in love, it can be invested in poverty or it can be invested in prosperity. The choice, of course, is ours. It is *we* who choose what we want to fill our lives.

A CASE OF INTELLECTUAL FAITH

Doctor Carl Simonton, a cancer radiologist, in his book *Getting Well Again*.[1] tells the story of a man with a virulent form of cancer—a lymphosarcoma. The man was gravely ill. He had huge tumor masses and needed fluid removal from his chest every other day. He frequently had to take oxygen by mask and could do little else but lie in bed. His physician was at that time involved in cancer research with a promising new drug called krebiozen. The man heard about the drug and about everyone's high expectations and begged to be treated with it. His physician complied and the man made a "startling" recovery. His tumors disappeared, his chest stopped filling up with fluid, he did not need extra amounts of oxygen, he got out of bed and he even began flying his private airplane again. He was symptom-free for two months.

Then some negative publicity began to be written about the drug. The news media started publishing reports about the failure of krebiozen in some preliminary tests. When this happened, the man's symptoms began reappearing. Before long he again had the massive tumors, the fluid-filled chest and the need for extra oxygen. He was bedridden and unable to work.

His physician became so concerned at this point that he decided to tell the man that he had received a new, improved, super-strength batch of the drug which was far superior to what he had formerly been using and he wanted to administer it to him. The man enthusiastically agreed and the new injections were initiated. This time, however,

1. Bantam Books, Inc., N.Y., 1980, pg. 22.

the injections were not krebiozen at all; they were merely *sterile water!*

But again the man made "remarkable" improvement. The tumor masses melted, there was no more fluid in the chest, no need for the oxygen mask and the man again returned to work and again began to fly his own private airplane.

A short time later the headlines in the newspaper read "Nationwide Test Shows Krebiozen to be Worthless in Treatment of Cancer." A few days later the man died.

Where had this man invested his faith? What was the mold he created for his faith to fill? Was his faith anchored in the Truth of his being—that he was whole and healthy—or was it an intellectual faith based only on what he could read and hear? "According to thy faith be it done unto you," and according to our faith it always is done unto us.

A CASE OF SPIRITUAL FAITH

Contrast that story with the story the great Nobel prize-winning physician Alexis Carrel tells of an incident which he scientifically observed and later wrote of in his book *The Voyage to Lourdes.*[2] The story deals with Dr. Carrel's journey, as a young physician, with a train-load of sick to the shrine at Lourdes, France. His intention was to learn whether or not the reports from Lourdes of radical improvements were authentic. During the trip some of the faithful on the train were so sick that Dr. Carrel was frequently called to minister to them on the way. He was kept especially busy with a girl named Marie—a young girl with what Carrel described as "a classic case of tubercular peritonitis." She had been ill with this particular condition for eight months. In fact, she was so ill and her condition so

2. Harper and Row, New York, 1950

precarious that her personal physician had refused to operate on her, considering her case "hopeless."

While on the train going to Lourdes, she went into a
coma on several occasions. It was only Dr. Carrel's medical intervention which saved her. In talking to the girl (and
later to her personal physician at home) Dr. Carrel found
out that both of her parents had died of tuberculosis. At
seventeen, she was already spitting blood and at eighteen
she had a tubercular pleurisy which required more than a
half gallon of fluid being drawn from her left lung. She
had pulmonary lesions and for the last eight months had
an unmistakable tubercular peritonitis.

Nevertheless the girl insisted that she wanted to be taken
to Lourdes. The pain which she had to endure on the
bumpy train ride was terrible but her faith was such that
she gladly bore it.

After arriving at Lourdes, Carrel was called again to
minister to the girl. This time he brought another physician
with him to examine her. They both agreed, "she is almost
completely wasted away. Her heart is racing madly (150
beats per minute and irregular). Look how thin she is.
Look at the color of her face and hands. She may last a few
more days, but she is doomed. Death is very near," Carrel
felt, "She may die any moment right under my nose. If she
gets home again alive, that in itself will be a miracle."

Marie was determined to be bathed in the water at
Lourdes. Her abdomen was so sore and her body so frail
that it was decided not to dip her in the water. Instead
water was poured over her abdomen. Dr. Carrel describes
the girl: "She lay on her back, all shrunken beneath the
dark brown blanket which made a mound over her distended abdomen. Her breath came quick and short. The
sick girl was apparently unconscious. Her pulse was more

rapid than ever. Her face was ashen. It was obvious that this young girl was about to die.'' But the girl did not die. In a matter of two hours after having the water poured over her the girl had lost all symptoms of her sickness! Dr. Carrel reported: ''She was cured. In the span of a few hours, a girl with a face already turning blue, a distended abdomen, and a fatally racing heart had been restored . . . to health.''

Jesus said, ''Thy faith hath made thee whole.'' It was Marie's faith which made her whole. The mold that Marie created for her faith to fill was modeled after the Truth of her being. Hers was a spiritual faith anchored in her divine essence and exercised deep within her spiritual consciousness. When faith is so anchored and so exercised it quickly finds its right place and under the law of mind action (like attracts like, like begets like) brings forth a manifestation which seems miraculous.

Such ''miracles'' are impossible with intellectual faith alone because the foundation of intellectual faith is in the shifting sands of circumstances and appearances. When the circumstances change our faith shifts and all that we have built on such faith crumbles.

Marie had faith that when she was bathed with the ''holy water'' she would get well. This was an intellectual faith, it is true, but Marie's faith went much further than this intellectual faith. Marie was aware that virtually everyone else who was bathed in the water with her showed no improvement! Imagine the deep, solid, well-rooted faith this girl must have had, seeing such failures and not being swayed. If her faith were only an intellectual faith based solely on appearances, it would have crumbled when faced with such overwhelming evidence of failure. But Marie's faith did not falter. The water was merely a catalyst which hastened the expression of a deeper, more spiritual faith which she possessed. Marie had complete confidence in her eventual good. This is true faith.

ACCORDING TO THY FAITH

The cancer patient in Dr. Simonton's book had a faith which was strictly and purely an intellectual faith. It was based *totally* on an appearance. Even after being given the drug krebiozen and becoming symptom-free for two months, his faith could not overcome the negative reports of the newsmedia. In an effort to convince him of his divine right to health the life force dwelling within him made him healthy again—this time without any help from a drug! But the man's faith was based on krebiozen and so he let the news of krebiozen's failure kill him.

Faith allows us to appropriate the spiritual substance of whatever it is we desire. When we do so we have taken the first important step necessary for manifesting our good. The man could not take this important first step and thus he doomed himself to failure. He could not even accept the inner evidence of his own body as proof of his health, so singularly was his faith attached to something in the outer.

To all outward appearances Marie was fatally ill and *her faith made her well*. To all outward appearances the man was well and *his faith made him fatally ill!*

IS FAITH ENOUGH?

In the Bible we read ". . . if you have faith as a grain of mustard seed, you will say to this mountain, 'Move hence to yonder place,' and it will move; and nothing will be impossible to you." If this is the case, why should we make any physical effort on our own behalf? Wouldn't it be easier to bring forth a desired manifestation in our lives merely by increasing our faith? The answer to this, of course, is a resounding *YES!* Our faith can make us whole. However, it is important to note two things. First of all, it takes a great deal of effort to expand our faith. It is true that we are given an unlimited amount of faith as part of our divine birthright, but it is incumbent on each of us to expand and invest that faith. And we can only do so by making an effort. Faith must be anchored in the firm foundation of deeds.

And secondly and most importantly, although our faith is infinitely expandable, *faith can only expand to the self-imposed boundaries of our present consciousness.* It can go no further. Our consciousness creates an artificial border which limits the infinite potential of our faith, and faith so limited can only express in a limited way.

How can our faith affirm the brotherhood of man and peace when our consciousness dictates that "this race is inferior?"

How can our faith in our abundant prosperity help but be limited when our consciousness affirms, "I'll never be able to afford that?"

How can our faith in our innate wholeness keep us healthy when our consciousness fears "the coming flu season?"

Faith can only expand to the self-imposed boundaries of our present consciousness! Jesus had a consciousness which expanded to the limitless reaches of His spirit. His faith, therefore, was limitless and the acts He performed thus seemed miraculous. But Jesus was able to perform them because He let Spirit flow uninhibitedly through His soul, expanding His consciousness without limit.

Are There "Higher" Laws?

Jesus did not use "higher" laws than physical laws when he healed the sick, calmed the seas or resurrected Himself from the dead. Jesus merely employed "other" laws that His expanded consciousness was able to perceive and His expanded faith able to utilize.

At one time man thought that the law of gravity was supreme and that he could never fly! But the laws of aerodynamics were finally discovered and heavier than air machines began flying in response to these laws. But does that mean that the laws of aerodynamics are "higher" laws than the law of gravity? Not at all; they are not higher laws, they are simply different laws—other laws. When flying, the airplane is responding to the laws of aerodynamics; when landing it is responding to the law of gravity. One law is not higher than the other. They are both equally valid. The pilot decides which law he wants to use and when he wants to use it. The choice is his.

In the same sense the laws which bring us sickness, poverty and hatred are just as equal and just as valid as those which bring health, prosperity and love. It is we who choose which laws we want to use and when we want to use them.

Substance responds to our faith in it. Our faith can be invested as strongly in sickness as in health, as strongly in poverty as in prosperity, as strongly in hatred as in love. The choice, of course, is always ours.

FILL THE SOUL WITH FAITH

As we make an effort to seek the kingdom of God, as we make an effort to contact our eternal, unchanging nucleus which is our constant source of inspiration, we will steadily expand our consciousness. And as we do our faith too will expand, always nudging at its boundaries, always anxious to spread into every corner of our unlimited soul and bring forth our most fervent desires.

We often try to do things "our way" only to find out that "our way" is the wrong way. But we have been given clear instructions for manifesting all that we desire and these instructions are actually quite simple. They are ". . . whatever you ask in prayer, *believe* that you receive it, and you will."

Substance responds to our faith in it. In God's realm our deepest desire is already fulfilled! Faith is the means by which we bring that desire from God's realm to our realm.

Chapter X

GOD'S TURN

Said the Robin to the Sparrow:
"I should really like to know
Why these anxious human beings
Rush about and worry so."

Said the Sparrow to the Robin:
"Friend, I think that it must be
That they have no heavenly Father
Such as cares for you and me."

Elizabeth Cheney

When we have earnestly taken the first six steps in our SOUL SURGERY we have done all that we can do to allow Spirit to flow unimpededly through us. Once we have become aware of our problem, blessed it, acted on our own behalf to remedy it and shown complete confidence in our eventual good then we can do nothing more! It is now GOD'S TURN.

The preceding steps were active steps. They required our active participation. Step seven requires nothing further from us because in step seven we "let go and let God." We "let go" of our doubts and anxieties and "let God" unfold His perfect good.

In step seven we say "good-bye" to our problem but, more importantly, *we also say "good-bye" to our involvement in that problem.* We don't outline our good and then when it is "past due" begin worrying about it. No, we get our minds off of the problem and onto the solution—God. And we don't let go *after* the problem is resolved. We let go *NOW!*

LET IT GO AND LET IT GROW

The ability to let go while we are doing all that we can do is essential because it allows our good to ripen naturally and fully. What kind of farmer would carefully prepare his soil, scrupulously select his seed, lovingly plant it and then dig it up every day to see if it were still growing? Our first six steps "planted the seed" of our good, now we must "let it grow."

SOUL SURGERY is designed to remove any obstacles which block the flow of spiritual inspiration through our soul. Once we have removed everything which inhibits this free flowing, we know that our problems and challenges will disappear. After we have done our share, the strongest faith we can show is to turn things over to God. When we do this we are showing faith in our faith! Letting go allows God to lead us along the safest, surest path. When we get ourselves out of the way we allow God to solve our problem. Our ultimate success lies not in us but in God.

If we are not able to let go and allow our good to unfold this is a sure sign that our faith is not fully expanded and that we must strengthen that faith. If we keep trying to force the solution ourselves and not put our faith in God, our faith will soon change to anxiety. Anxiety is fear projected into the future and fear is the most successful inhibitor of our good. When we become anxious we will no longer be an open channel. We will have blocked the flow of our blessings. If we *dwell* on our problem we are, in effect, *affirming* it and each time we affirm it we give it more dominion over us.

Once we are doing all that we can do on our own behalf and, with faith, put ourselves in the hands of God, we must never take matters back into our own hands. In doing so we simply push our good further off into the future.

No Time Limit

Let's be careful not to put a time limit on God. Let's not let doubt detour our faith. It is easy to become anxious when our good does not manifest according to *our* time schedule. If we want God to take charge of our life we must let go of all doubts, anxieties, worries and fear. We must stop dwelling on the difficulty and begin dwelling on the solution—God! When we can do this and put aside these doubts and fears our faith will again resurface and expand and our deliverance will soon follow.

Gratitude Affirms Faith

In our quiet moments a part of us whispers of a Power within which is greater than us and which will make us whole and healthy if we will just not deny it. If when faced with a negative situation we are able to tune in to this voice and say, "I am grateful for my eventual good," we will have proclaimed a powerful affirmation, one which will greatly quicken and expand our faith. Such gratitude, if it is felt deeply and said sincerely, is a sure indication to us that we have let go of our problem and released it to a higher power. Conversely, if we cannot deeply and sincerely feel this gratitude, we know that there is an aspect of us which is still holding on.

Before Jesus raised Lazarus from the tomb where Lazarus had been for four days, He said "Father, *I thank you* for you have heard me, And I know that you always hear me . . ." John 11:41 (Emphasis added.) in other words, *before* His desire was granted, Jesus showed gratitude as if it already had been accomplished! His sincere gratitude before any evidence of success showed His unlimited faith and His unlimited faith assured His unqualified success.

Gratitude, therefore, can be a useful barometer of our faith. Our ability or inability to say "thank you for my good" *before* our good is manifest indicates to us the depth of our faith. The more deeply and sincerely felt our gratitude is, the firmer and more productive our faith has become. Like a bird that trusts God to bring the dawn, we must begin singing while it is still dark.

If we cannot show gratitude, if we cannot honestly say "thank you, Father," we must reconsider the steps we have taken thus far and try to ascertain why our faith is so shallow.

RELEASE IT ALL

Many of us who are capable of releasing every other problem in our lives have a great deal of difficulty when it comes to letting go of a sickness. There are often parts of our mind which do not want us to get well. We delude ourselves into believing, "I'd better keep my hands off my suffering, it's all I have."

We may feel that if we were to let go of our sickness it would be gone and that without it we would have nothing. Our sickness may give us a chance to get some attention—

some sympathy or some love that we feel we otherwise could not get. Of course these considerations may not be conscious ones. As far as we are concerned we want to get well! However, when it comes time for releasing our sickness and giving it to God, we just cannot do it. But our very inability to release our sickness should serve to show us that there is some aspect of it which we think our soul needs. It should alert us to the fact that our awareness must deepen further so that we can discover this need and work to remove it.

REACH FOR YOUR GOOD

We can never climb to a higher rung of a ladder until we first let go of a lower one. We can never climb up to our good unless we first let go of our difficulties.

It's very much like a trapeze "flyer" swinging back and forth high above the sawdust of the circus center ring. All eyes are upon him as the audience waits for him to perform his famous trick. Across from him, swinging patiently, is his catcher, anxious to do his part in making the trick a success. Everything is ready. The flyer has a great desire to perform the trick, he has put great effort into his practicing and outwardly expresses faith in literally putting himself in the hands of his catcher. He professes complete faith that the catcher will be at the proper place at the proper time, able to catch him and not drop him. But the flyer continues swinging back and forth, firmly grasping his trapeze, unable to let go! How can he possibly expect to perform his act if he will not let go of his trapeze? The fact is that he cannot. Obviously the first step for the flyer to take after preparing himself as best he can is letting go of his trapeze. Unless he does that he will certainly fail to reach his goal.

Release is essential for completion. And the release must be *total*. The flyer cannot put half of his trust in his trapeze and the other half in the catcher. He cannot swing out toward the catcher, grabbing one of the catcher's hands while holding on to his own trapeze with the other! No, the flyer can reach his goal, he can complete his act, only by showing complete faith in his catcher. And this means *totally* releasing his trapeze.

LET GOD

If you have taken the first six steps in SOUL SURGERY and are currently swinging back and forth, afraid to let go, then you are restricting and delaying your good. You must eventually make the decision to release your problem and put yourself in the hands of God. When you finally let go and place yourself in the mighty hands that support the universe, it at last becomes GOD'S TURN.

Chapter XI

PROGNOSIS

If we obey God's laws, we fit perfectly into the divine mosaic of universal perfection and we experience that perfection in all phases of our life.

SOUL IS EMANCIPATED

The seven steps of SOUL SURGERY do not *make* something happen. Rather, by freeing the soul of false beliefs, they *prepare our consciousness* to accept the good that is ours by divine right. Each step that we take—from our initial AWARENESS to our allowing GOD'S TURN—results in more and more of our good's being expressed in our lives and in our affairs.

Remember that our spirit is always perfect because all the characteristics of the God-Mind are in it. Inspiration from the spirit is always flowing through us but it is *we* who determine whether it will be a torrent or a trickle. As long as we allow any false beliefs based on mere appearances to rule our consciousness these beliefs become barriers and effectively dam our good. Only a removal of these false beliefs can open the floodgate of gifts which are in store for us when the soul receives inspiration from our spirit.

And if inspiration from the spirit is to flow unimpededly through our souls then *all* areas of the soul must be free. It is illogical to think that spirit can express through us as perfect health when, for instance, we feel hatred or unforgiveness. Such feelings of hate not only block spirit from expressing as perfect love, they restrict spirit from expressing as perfect health, as happiness, as abundance, as all good in our lives.

BODY REFLECTS SOUL

If we are to mirror our spirit in body and outer affairs we can only do so when we reflect *all* aspects of our Christ nature. If we leave out one aspect or if we cannot express it as fully as does our spirit, then we are not a true reflection.

We cannot paint a picture of a rainbow without the color red, can we? Nor can we leave out orange or yellow or green or blue or indigo or violet. Without all of these colors we would not be expressing a rainbow because a rainbow can only express as the full spectrum of *all* colors.

The abundance of God expresses as a complete spectrum of good. When we have opened our soul to channel *all* of this good we will then reflect our perfection. We can never *fully* express in any area unless *all* areas are free. And *the abundance we express in all areas is limited by the area we express the least.*

For example, as we've seen, hatred will block love from flowing into our life. However, if we are successful in overcoming that hatred we will not only receive more love, we will also demonstrate better health, more prosperity and greater happiness. Our hatred will not have inhibited only our expression of love, it will have restricted our good in *all* areas. To the extent that we are able to overcome hatred and express love we will be able to express all of God's gifts.

KEEP YOUR CONSCIOUSNESS CLEAR

SOUL SURGERY changes our consciousness. And in changing our consciousness it releases us from our problems and prepares us for our good. But unless our consciousness *remains* changed problems will always return. Unless we can sustain the freedom from false beliefs which have led to our deliverance we run the risk of having our consciousness attract back to us the same or similar situations as before. Perhaps the names of those involved will change or our ailments will strike a different organ in the body but trouble, in some form, will be back in our lives unless we keep our consciousness clear.

It is important to remember that what we are—what we manifest in our life—is always exactly the outpicturing of what our soul has apprehended from our spirit. That is why many faith healings are temporary. The ardor and excitement of the moment, the tentative anticipation of a healing, the deeply stirring influence of the crowd, the exciting sounds of the uplifting music, the suggestive preachings about the power of God to heal—all of these combine to expand faith to such a degree that the consciousness is also expanded. In this expanded state of consciousness the soul is able to discern in spirit the divine blueprint of health and wholeness. The body, therefore, responds by claiming this perfection. The healing is consummated. Sickness is no more.

But after the drama of the event is over, after the people return to their daily routines and are again subjected to the outer influences which affected their lives before their miraculous cure, it's so easy for their old consciousness to return, effectively constricting their good and bringing back into their lives whatever problems they had before.

Having used SOUL SURGERY to change our lives we must be very careful to guard our consciousness from any delusive doctrines, any malignant maxims, any false beliefs which would re-attach themselves to our soul and constrict the outpouring of our good.

DOES IT FIT?

Now that the entire operation of SOUL SURGERY has been explained and you have a better understanding of how it can lead to your personal self-healing, you can more easily personalize it to fit your specific problem—to answer your personal need.

An important thing to remember about SOUL SURGERY is that in order for it to work for you, you must feel comfortable with it. If it doesn't feel comfortable you won't want to attempt it. Or, having begun it, you may not want to continue working with it.

The order in which the seven steps appear is not an arbitrary one. This specific sequence has proven to work best for most people. However, you may feel that it doesn't suit your personal needs. You may feel more comfortable with a different order, one which meets your requirements better than this one.

If you have given serious thought to changing the sequence of SOUL SURGERY and you feel good about doing it, then by all means do it!

ONE AT A TIME OR ALL AT ONCE?

Some people take each step of SOUL SURGERY separately, not going on to the next until they entirely complete that step. Others work on all of the steps at once. But the operation is usually most effective when each step is begun separately *and then* is continued throughout all of the other steps. For example, just because AWARENESS is the first step doesn't mean that after you take this first step you must abandon it. Your awareness often deepens as you continue your SOUL SURGERY. And as it deepens you are able to get closer and closer to the solution of your problem. SOUL SURGERY is much more effective when you keep your mind open and allow each subsequent step to expand that awareness.

And just because you have given the problem your BLESSING in Step Two doesn't necessarily mean that you should forget about blessing it again merely because you are on another step. It never hurts to bless it no matter where you are in your SOUL SURGERY.

And when you give your problem to God—when it's finally GOD'S TURN— don't think that you should stop working on your problem; don't think that your efforts should cease. Not at all. Continuing to do all that you can on your own behalf, you now allow God to answer your deeds as *He* sees fit, not as you think He should see fit. You continue affirming "Thy will be done," releasing your concern but *not relinquishing your efforts or ceasing to continue the other steps.*

The same holds true with all of the steps. Your having performed them does not necessarily mean that you can forget about them. In this way your operation attains a cumulative effect, which grows stronger with each step.

THERE IS ALWAYS AN ANSWER

No problem is without a solution. No situation is hopeless. No trouble is terminal. Whatever machinations led us into our present plight will be immediately reversed to lead us out of it as soon as we take the proper steps to do so. There is good in *every* situation. All exists in creation and therefore all is one with creation. The Creative Force responsible for our existence can only know Itself through Its creations. It can only express through Its creations and Its expression, therefore, can only be directed toward Its own good. The Creative Force is not in conflict with Itself.

EACH STEP IMPORTANT

In SOUL SURGERY we actively prepare our consciousness to become passive—to become open, receptive and secure in the absolute knowledge that our good is on the way. The seven steps are designed to uncover our perfection. Each step is important because each step takes us closer to that perfection, adding something to our ability to claim it.

AWARENESS alerts us.
BLESSING prepares us.
COMMITMENT motivates us.
DENIALS and AFFIRMATIONS convince us.
EFFORT involves us.
FAITH sustains us.
GOD'S TURN delivers us.

PROGNOSIS: ETERNAL LIFE

The body is soul expressing. When we allow our perfect spirit to *fully* express its infinite abundance and inspiration through our *unlimited* soul, then that spirit will manifest its perfection in our body. Perfect spirit flowing through unrestricted soul becomes perfect body. Spirit, soul and body express as one and thus become one.

SOUL SURGERY, therefore, will have taken us from a diagnosis of "impediment in the soul, blocking the flow of good" to a prognosis of "eternal life," for in the fusing of spirit, soul and body into one, we discover that at last we have become one with the ONE.

SOUL SURGERY

Part Two

WORKBOOK

PREFACE TO THE WORKBOOK

This workbook is to be used in conjunction with the text *SOUL SURGERY: The Ultimate Self-Healing*. In it are listed effective and realistic suggestions which are designed to complement the more theoretical ideas of the text. By working step-by-step with these practical guidelines you will be able to perform your own life-transforming operation—your own self-healing—so that your soul can be freed of any obstacles which may be threatening or inhibiting your expression of perfection.

In addition to the special instructions for each of the seven steps, the workbook deals with five general categories into which the vast majority of our problems fall. It not only shows how each step of SOUL SURGERY can be specifically applied to these common challenges, it also gives examples of how SOUL SURGERY has helped others.

Most of the problems which we encounter in our lives will fall into one or more of these five general categories:

1) HEALTH—Challenges in the area of health include any problem which is causing the body or mind to manifest anything less than its perfection and is causing any pain, discomfort, anxiety or fear.

These problems can be "major" diseases such as cancer, heart disease, arthritis, diabetes and many others. But "minor" maladies like frequent headaches, chronic upset stomach, allergies, mental problems, backaches, bad gums and constipation can be just as depressing to the one affected as the most serious disease. (The life of a woman who makes her living selling cosmetics, for example, may be more affected by a stubborn skin rash on her face than someone else's life might be by diabetes!)

We will not address ourselves to the degree of seriousness of a problem. The terms "major" sickness and "minor" sickness are really relative terms. The fact of the matter is that if there is *any* challenge to our health it must be explored because it indicates a blockage in the soul.

2) PROSPERITY—This category deals with lack, whether it be lack of money, lack of a satisfying job, lack of ambition, lack of a suitable place to live, or lack of anything you feel you really desire but for some reason haven't been able to obtain.

3) PERSONAL RELATIONSHIPS—This deals with the area of LOVE. It is the category which concerns itself with relationships which are keeping you from showing your true Christ self. It could be a "troublesome" mother-in-law, a "hateful" boss, a "spiteful" neighbor, a "selfish" child or an "unloving" mate. It covers, in essence, any situation in which there is a person whom you have

trouble loving and/or whom you feel has trouble loving you.

4) DOMINION—This category deals with any challenge you have with either a person or a substance which you "can't resist." Some obvious examples in the area of DOMINION are alcohol, drugs and tobacco, which can easily become habitual if you allow them. But also included in this category can be food, which many an obese person has difficulty controlling, and gambling, which can often become addictive.

You allow something dominion over you when you let your fears and phobias control you. A fear of elevators or flying or confined places may be just as much a loss of control as alcoholism!

DOMINION also includes the power you give events or to the position of the stars and planets to dictate your life.

And finally, this category encompasses those situations where you have allowed another person to dominate your thoughts and actions, controlling you according to his or her idea of how you should act.

In all of these situations you are not your own master—you do not completely control your own fate, you have surrendered a portion of your freedom. You are in bondage! When you have given something domnion over you, you are in bondage to that thing. It controls you; you do not control it.

If you "*must have* another drink," or "*can't live* without my cigarettes," or "will *never* get into that elevator," or if you find yourself saying he "*made me* do it," or she "*makes me* so angry," or "I'm a Gemini and Geminis are just not good at . . . ," then you are in bondage! You are not truly free.

5) CONCERN FOR ANOTHER PERSON—This deals with wanting to help a loved one whom, you feel, is not doing the proper thing and is "messing up his life," or whom you feel is suffering unfairly.

This includes the son who is on drugs, the daughter who is traveling with the wrong group of boys, the husband who can't seem to control his alcohol consumption, the sister who is beaten and abused by her mate, the good friend who is fighting a battle with cancer. In each of these cases you are concerned for another person. In other words, you have taken *his* problem and made it *your* problem.

These five general categories are by no means exhaustive. These are by no means all of the problems we can face, but these five cover the great majority of human concerns and challenges.

We will examine each of the seven steps of SOUL SURGERY in the context of these separate categories. In each chapter of this workbook you can locate the category which best fits your challenge and work with that one. Although it is not necessary to study the other four categories, it is often very helpful to do so.

Lesson One

INTRODUCTION

To be used in conjunction with Chapters I, II, and III of the text.

Every soul has its secrets. Many times these secrets prove to be the very obstacles which are preventing us from being our real selves. We know now that these obstacles must be removed forever if we are to move ahead in consciousness and express perfection in our lives and affairs.

Uncovering, identifying and excising the soul hindrances, therefore, is a highly personal task. Your soul is uniquely your own. You alone traverse its peaks and valleys. You alone have traveled into its dark crevasses and across its sunlit meadows. You alone have built its prisons as well as its cathedrals.

You do not know what route your soul has taken down through time, but you *do* know that whatever it is today is a direct result of that route. Your soul today is a boundless road atlas pinpointing all of the experiences, all of the beliefs, all of the thoughts and feelings which it has chosen to retain from the past. Many of these beliefs have caused and are still causing you to detour or chase down dead-ends, diverting you from your good.

You can see by now that the more obstacles clinging to your soul—and the larger they are—the more retarded will be the flow of spirit into your body and outer affairs.

These obstacles must be painstakingly removed, one-by-one. Eventually all of them must go, but at the moment there is probably one major obstacle which dominates all others. This is the big problem in your life. This is the one you will operate on now.

Remember, in SOUL SURGERY you are working with that perfection within yourself. You will be drawing on a creative Power which is *already* part of you. This Power is there for you to use. In fact, since a creator can only know itself through its creations, It *longs* for you to use It so that It can express more of Itself! At this very moment that Power within promises you the same deliverance as It did ty Cyrus in the book of Isaiah: "I will go before thee, and make the crooked places straight: I will break in pieces the gates of brass, and cut in sunder the bars of iron: and I will give thee the treasures of darkness, and hidden riches of secret places."

That is God's personal prmise to you too! SOUL SURGERY is an effective means of your allowing God to keep that promise.

Lesson Two

AWARENESS

To be used in conjunction with Chapter IV of Text.

We cannot search for a solution if we don't know what it is we are trying to solve. Define your problem. What is it in your life which you want to remove? State very definitely what the challenge is. This is an important step. Don't put off doing it any longer. Write it out today—NOW! Be specific.

"My problem is _____."

"I want _____ removed from my life."

THE ULTIMATE CAUSE

Now that you think you have correctly stated your problem, let's examine the four causes of a problem to help us determine what the real obstruction on the soul is. As covered in the text, the four causes of any event are its *external cause, obvious cause, essential cause* and *ultimate cause*. To quickly review, the *external cause* of a church, for instance, is the walls, the pews, the pulpit and so on. The *obvious cause* of a church would be the workers who built it—the masons, the carpenters, the electricians, plumbers and others. The *essential cause* of the church is the blueprint drawing by the architect which the workers followed. But the *ultimate cause* of the church is the need for a place to worship.

Any problem in your life can be outlined according to these four causes. It is your responsibility to discover your ultimate cause and to remove it. This is done by searching the soul through self-introspection and meditation. Have you done this yet? It not, begin today to identify these causes.

HEALTH

Before you can overcome your problem you must first be aware that you have one. This awareness comes easiest in the area of health. If you have pain or discomfort, you know you have a problem! It is you who are closest to your own body and when something is not working properly you are usually the first to know.

The next step in AWARENESS is to trace the cause of pain or sickness back to its *real* source. (Even a problem like constipation is caused *first* by a blockage in the soul before it becomes a blockage in the bowels.) Begin with identifying the external cause and then the obvious cause. Next, work your way through identifying the essential cause until you finally confront the ultimate cause. Why are you sick? Why do you need your sickness? *How would you act if you were suddenly well?* The closer you can get to these answers, the easier your problem will be to overcome.

A woman with crippling arthritis in her legs spent most of her time in a wheelchair. The external cause was the disability termed "arthritis." The obvious cause was the pain and swelling. The essential cause was her erroneous belief that she inherited arthritis from her mother who had it. But her *ultimate* cause proved to be her soul's need for loving attention and sympathy which the condition forced her husband and family to provide.

Illness can often be used as a means to gain attention and loving care. This is an unfair method of trying to attain what would otherwise freely and joyfully be given to one whose soul is free enough to let love flow through it. To use illness in order to obtain a love that is already ours is like robbing a bank to obtain money which is in our account!

What is the need in your soul which is causing it to bring forth a dis-ease in the physical body? Why does your soul have such a need? If you have tried your best and cannot find the ultimate cause of your problem, don't agonize over it. Let it go and continue on to the next step. Sooner or later the ultimate cause will pop out of your subconscious and reveal itself to you.

PROSPERITY

A young salesman failed at every job he held. He never could earn enough to feel comfortable. The external cause of his lack was the absence of a good salary. The obvious cause was his lackluster sales. The essential cause was his erroneous belief that he was an inept salesman and therefore doomed to poverty. But he found that the *ultimate* cause was his soul's need to carry out the "programming" it received as a child, when his poverty-stricken parents indoctrinated him with the idea that it was his lot to be poor just as they always were.

You were not created to be poor in anything. If you feel poor you can be sure that something is blocking the flow of riches into your life. Ask yourself, "Do I need my poverty?" "Is lack of success filling a special area in my life that nothing else can satisfy?" "If I were prosperous would I feel uncomfortable?" *"Would I feel guilty if I were rich?"* Think deeply on each of these questions—especially the last one! They are important in helping you to become aware of your *real* problem.

Remember that poverty is a symptom and not a cause. Poverty is serving the purpose of your soul right now. Can you locate the need in your soul which is causing you to demonstrate financial lack in your life? Where did this need come from in the first place? If you had such a need in the past do you still have the same need now? Try to find the essential cause and the ultimate cause. Find out why you need it. Take this question into meditation and open yourself up to divine guidance for the answer. After you ask for help, *listen* for the answer. A still, small voice within you will always tell you all you want to know—*but you can hear it only when you listen.*

PERSONAL RELATIONSHIPS

A very possessive widow felt that the warm love between her and her only child was destroyed when he married a girl of whom she vehemently disapproved. She felt "crushed" and lonely when he had moved out of the house, thinking that the only important person in her life didn't love her any more.

The external cause of her unhappiness was the lack of a meaningful relationship with her son. The obvious cause was his marriage to a girl she did not approve of. The essential cause was the erroneous belief that because the son was married he could not still love his mother as much as before. However, the *ultimate* cause was her soul's need to possess those things that she loved. This insecurity was caused by losing her own parents at an early age and the death of her husband after only a few years of marriage.

If there is hatred in your life—either hatred *by* you or hatred *of* you—then you have a serious problem. And the problem is not the hatred itself. Don't confuse the symptom with the cause. If you are experiencing a lack of love, then you can be sure that something is constricting love from pouring through you. Remove the obstruction and love will again flow freely, your life and affairs changing to mirror this abundant love.

Are you able to identify the reason why an abundance of love is not forthcoming? Remember, blaming someone else is *not* identifying the reason. If someone is acting hatefully toward you, if you are lonely, if you feel unloved, if there are any problems with love's expressing in your life, be sure of one thing: it is because of something *you* are doing. Don't fall into the trap of externalizing the blame, no matter how righteously you feel you are acting. It's too easy to assign to someone else the reason for our misery. The fact is that you have allowed this problem into your life for a reason—because it is serving a need. Try to become aware of what that need is so that it can be satisfied in a more positive way.

Consider your own personal relationship challenge. When did it begin? Why? What need does your soul have which makes you act the way you do? Why? Why? And still why?

It is often difficult to probe the consciousness so minutely that you find every hidden need—every hidden blockage. If you have tried and are still puzzled as to why you can't claim your rightful inheritance of love, don't agonize over it, simply go to the next step aware, at least, that there *is* a blockage and that you will eventually find and remove it.

DOMINION

A successful attorney became addicted to alcohol and his work was starting to suffer. The external cause of his problem was the alcoholism itself. The obvious cause was his excessive consumption of alcohol. The essential cause was his erroneous belief that drinking eases tensions and helps one to forget his cares. The *ultimate* cause was his soul's need for the extra love, attention and concern that he felt his wife, family and friends showed for him when he was intoxicated. This grew out of his feelings of lack of love as a child of stern and unfeeling parents.

What is it which you feel has dominion over you? Are you willing to ask "why" until you get to the bottom line of the problem? What do you see in your soul's experience which could have created a need for this substance or person to have dominion over you?

The first thing to recognize is that if something in your life does have control over you it did not *take* control—you *gave it* control. *Freedom is not lost, it is surrendered!* If you have surrendered your freedom you should be aware that you can claim it back again—and you can do it any time you wish.

But more importantly, try to become aware of *why* you have given up your freedom. Why do you drink or smoke or overeat? Why are you afraid of confined places or airplanes? Why have you allowed someone or something to control your life? What special need are these things satisfying that nothing else can? Try to answer this question.

Are the alcohol or drugs a substitute for the love you feel is lacking in your life? Are the phobias really fears of death? Do you allow dominance because you are afraid to make certain decisions for yourself? Try to become aware of the *real* reason these problems exist.

You can overcome these addictions, phobias, fears and dependencies. You will do so when you realign yourself with the Spirit within you. Give control of your life to a higher power by transferring dominion from substance to Spirit. *The more you depend on Spirit, the less you need depend on substance!*

CONCERN FOR ANOTHER PERSON

A father was heartbroken when he discovered his teen-aged son was on hard drugs. He wanted desperately to help him. The external cause of the man's problem was his despair and frustration at seeing his son "do this to his life." The obvious cause of the problem was the boy's taking drugs. The essential cause was his erroneous belief that anything someone else did could inflict disaster on his own life. But the *ultimate* cause in this case was the father's personal need for love. He construed the approval of the community as love and felt that this approval—this "love" —was jeopardized by his son's actions. The father's need for social acceptability arose as a result of his having a father who was the "town drunk" and of whom he had always been ashamed.

Any negative situation presenting itself to you, whether it is in your life or in your affairs, is an indication that something in your soul is constricting your good. The fact that the problem is not with you but with a loved one makes no difference. If you have allowed it to affect *you* then you have made it *your* problem. It is now affecting *your* life. It is fulfilling a need in you and, therefore, the first thing you should do is find out why you feel the need to be so affected.

Examine your own soul. What is it in you that wants this person to change? Be honest. Is it the embarrassment he is causing you? Is there jealousy involved? Does resentment play any part? Certainly you love the person but is that the only motivation for your concern? True love is freeing, not constricting. True love allows the person to express himself in any way he desires. True love is not judgmental nor is it critical.

If you are greatly worried over a loved one be aware that this worry indicates an area in your own soul which must be freed. Naturally we feel love and concern for those close to us. We want to see them manifesting only good. The only thing we can do to help another, however, is to "hold him in the light." See him as perfect and filled with joy. That is our main responsibility to others.

If we feel our "problem" is due to someone else's actions or someone else's problem, we had better examine our real reason for these feelings. Sometimes we will be very surprised to uncover layers upon layers of needs in our own soul.

The truth is that others do not have the power to affect our lives unless we want them to. And then we must ask "why?" "Why have *I* brought this problem into *my* life?" "Why am I using someone else's soul needs to bring myself suffering?" "What is the need in my own soul which seeks this experience?"

THINGS TO DO

I) Set aside time each day for regular meditation so that you will become aware of your soul's needs. Try for one twenty minute session in the morning and another at night.

II) Analyze the causes of your problem.

A) External Cause. (State it simply and succinctly.)
   1. "My problem is _____."

B) Obvious Cause
   2. "This problem is due to _____."

C) Essential Cause
   1. "I am manifesting this problem because of my erroneous belief that _____."

D) Ultimate Cause
   1. "The real cause of this problem is my soul's need for _____."
   or
   2. "My soul has had need of this because _____."

III) Contact your LIFE GUIDE

In order to help us to identify the ultimate cause of our problem it is often helpful to go within to the "unconscious" part of our minds for the answer. This aspect of our mind—our unconscious (so called by Freud)—contains rich personal resources which we can mobilize for our own positive personal growth. This "center" deep within our psyche is full of information and is constantly sending us messages which are *always* directed toward our own well-being.

Since this center is outside of our conscious awareness, our unconscious communicates with us in a unique way. It uses the "language" of dreams and of feelings and of intuition. Unfortunately, we are taught early in life that such information is unscientific and unreliable and should therefore be disregarded as being of no consequence. And so these "still, small voices" go unheard, these "warnings" go unheeded, this rich vein of inner knowledge, awareness and healing goes virtually untapped.

But you *can* tap these resources. You can communicate with this center in you—with this personal problem solver, with this LIFE GUIDE. It will take a little practice and patience but the rewards in personal awareness and growth from this contact are enormous.

Although all of us have a Life Guide deep within our unconscious, each of us will image this Life Guide in a different way. To some their Life Guide will be an authority figure—a respected doctor, a sagacious philosopher, a revered historical religious figure. To others it may be a whimsical figure like a wise old owl or turtle or rabbit. It can take any form. Although each figure is different for each person, every Life Guide is speaking to us from that wise, intuitive part of our brain. Don't consciously think of what form your Life Guide will take. Let it appear spontaneously by using the technique that follows.

A) LIFE GUIDE Mental Imagery Process

1) Sit comfortably in a straight back chair and prepare yourself by using a suitable relaxation technique to quiet your body. (Do not lie down.)

2) After you are physically relaxed, image yourself as clearly as possible in a peaceful, serene and comfortable setting—either a place you know or one from your fantasies that you can *vividly* imagine. BE THERE!

3) Now notice a bright light coming toward you. (The light can be any color that does not alarm you. Many prefer a white, bluish-white or golden color.) As the light approaches you do *not* feel threatened, in fact you anticipate your good from it.

4) As the glowing light comes closer you notice that it is a living creature—either a person whom you do not personally know or an animal which you consider friendly. Look at the creature carefully. Notice details. If it is a person, is it male or female? What is the color of the skin, hair, eyes? How tall is he or she? What kind of clothes is the person wearing? If it is an animal, notice as much as you can about it. *See all the details as clearly as possible.* Take your time on this step.

5) If you feel comfortable and safe, if you have a very warm feeling toward this creature, then you know that you have contacted your Life Guide. (If you don't get

these feelings, dismiss the creature, say goodbye and watch it go back to where it came from.)

6) Ask your Life Guide's name. (It already knows your name and everything else about you!)

7) Get acquainted. Have a conversation with your Life Guide. Speak to it as you would a friend (you'll never find a closer friend!) Then ask it to help you to find the ULTIMATE CAUSE of your problem (or discuss any other problem with it).

8) Your guide may speak to you, it may use gestures, it may point to things, it may use symbols or objects to give you advice. *Everything the Life Guide does or says has an important meaning.* PAY CAREFUL ATTENTION.

9) When you feel the conversation is over, mutually agree as to how and when you will make contact in the future. BE VERY SPECIFIC!

10) Say goodbye to your Life Guide and slowly let your consciousness return to your present surroundings.

If you can't make contact with your Life Guide right away, don't be unduly discouraged. Remember, this is a part of you that you have disregarded for many years. The channels of communication may be rusty but they are still there and will eventually open. Be patient, it often takes several attempts before the Life Guide appears.

And don't feel embarrassed by consulting your Life Guide. The figure you are communicating with is merely a symbol for your own inner self. It is that wise, intuitive part of you with which you have been out of touch. When you are talking to your Life Guide, you are actually talking to yourself but not to your logical, rational, intellectual, verbal self. Instead, you are talking to that intuitive, feeling self.

When you can establish a meaningful relationship with your Life Guide, you will receive an amazing amount of information and advice about your life. If you listen carefully, your Life Guide will tell you why you've been making yourself poor or sick or unloved or any other challenge you are currently facing, and it will suggest what you can do to help yourself out of it.

Your Life Guide is a wonderful means of contacting that aspect of your brain—the right hemisphere—which is concerned with symbolic, intuitive functions. Use this guide regularly to expand your awareness and you will always be in contact with an important aspect of your *real* self.

Lesson Three

BLESSING

To be used in conjunction with Chapter V of the Text.

We have learned that every situation or condition—every seeming "problem"—contains within itself the seed of our good. When we bless a problem as a source of our forthcoming good, we are actually "watering" the seed so that it can germinate, grow and eventually blossom into that good!

Are you able to bless your problem? Sometimes this may seem to be a foolish and illogical thing to do. But it is not. Blessing is an act of faith and that alone makes it a worthwhile endeavor. But more than that, you bless your problem because it has led you to a greater awareness of your present limitations. Any meaningful attempt at blessing your challenge will soon prove to you just how effective this second step of SOUL SURGERY can be. It begins your deliverance. It is the first phase of release. It is your initial contact with your good.

HEALTH

Bless that pain and sickness! It is an indication that something is blocking your good—not only in the area of health—but in all areas. If it weren't for your sickness you might not know about that blockage and would not be able to take steps to remove it.

Blessing prepares you to receive your good. By blessing it you are claiming your good from it. "Thank you, sickness. I claim my good from you. You have taught me a great lesson and I am grateful. You can go now; you are no longer needed."

Blessing a part of your body which needs help is essential to healing. (Of course, blessing something does not mean dwelling on it! *The healing and renewing life force is automatically denied to all who dwell on their maladies.*) When you bless and love a portion of your tissues, you are activating the creative energies of the life force within those cells. Speaking words of encouragement to a part of the body is very helpful in restoring proper function. And expressing thanks for the God which is in the midst of you is a most direct way of enabling His healing power to flow through you.

A woman with a large tumor was able to bless those cells for showing her that she needed to work on her consciousness—in her case she needed to show more forgiveness. After blessing and thanking those cells she released them—they were no longer needed! She then blessed the life force within her, releasing it to do its perfect healing and renewing work. Of course the growth was eventually reduced to nothing. God was in the midst of her seeming dis-ease. Blessing and loving are extremely powerful activities.

PROSPERITY

By blessing the good that we already have we help it to increase. If your wallet or your bank account seems less full than you would like, do not condemn your lack. Condemnation is praise in the negative and, as we know, what we praise we increase. Therefore, if we condemn our lack of funds, we will increase our lack of funds! Condemnation and criticism can only decrease our good. That is why it's always so important to dwell on the positive.

Lovingly bless the good which is already yours and the good which is soon to be yours. There are no limits to the abundance of this universe except those which we ourselves impose. Bless your good, knowing that all your needs will be met.

Bless your money as you send it forth to do its work, whether it be payment of an electric bill or payment for a pair of shoes. When you bless your money its value is multiplied. Blessing your finances puts you back in the flow of prosperity.

If you have been clutching onto whatever finances you have, begrudging every payment and expenditure, try blessing instead. Try to go from an attitude of the closed fist of grasping to the extended hand of giving. And bless, bless, bless abundance into your life.

PERSONAL RELATIONSHIPS

Your enemies, or the people who stand in opposition to you, perfectly mirror your own faults. As clearly as an X-ray, your enemies show you exactly what areas of your soul need surgery. Those who stand in conflict with you are like a blueprint showing you where in your structure the weaknesses lie.

In that sense, because your enemies give you a warning about yourself, you must bless them and thank them for acting as channels of your good. And in blessing them and blessing the situation, you are releasing yourself from that person or situation, opening yourself up to allow your good to come to you.

Bless the negative situation—thank your "enemies" for being the channel of your good. "Thank you for reflecting me back to myself and for being a channel of my good."

If you don't bless them, you have allowed that "problem person" in your life to become your jailer! Hatred is a jail which restricts *only* those who hate. And there is really only one way to escape from this jail—you must love your way out! LOVE IS THE GREAT EMANCIPATOR. Love this person, bless this situation because it contains the seed of so much growth for you. When you are loving, when you are blessing, you are operating from your perfect center and this can bring only right actions and good results for *all* concerned.

That person—this situation—is bringing you untold opportunities for unfoldment and soul growth. How could you possibly not want to send forth your blessings? Think about it.

If you have trouble blessing that person, look very closely for the sign which he has hanging around his neck. Often it is difficult to see this sign but it is *always* there on every person, at every moment. It is even on you! This sign, which hangs often half-hidden from view under a plethora of self-defenses, fears, anxieties and insecurities, reads "PLEASE, LOVE ME." As you begin looking at this troublesome person in your life more and more with eyes of love, the sign becomes more and more evident. Love is our greatest need. We all crave it. And when you remind yourself that the sign is always there on everyone, no matter how hidden or faded it is, then it is easy to let your love flow in response to it.

Always remember to look for the sign, practice seeing it on everyone—especially on that special "problem person" in your life. Become aware that the more despicably a person acts toward you, the more he is pointing to that sign on his chest begging you "PLEASE, LOVE ME."

DOMINION

The most difficult thing for you to do may be to bless that which controls you. You are probably so disgusted by the trouble it seems to be causing that you don't even want to think about it. But, remember, *every* situation in which you find yourself contains the seed of your good. Blessing the situation plants that seed so that your good can grow.

The addiction or fear or domination shows you very clearly that your soul is not free to express your spirit fully and freely. Isn't that valuable information? With that knowledge you can now begin to do something about it—to free yourself of your self-imposed limitations.

Bless and release your lack of freedom, knowing that it has sown its useful purpose and can now go out of your life.

Bless a glass of whiskey? Bless a pack of cigarettes? Bless a bottle of drugs? Not exactly. But you do bless the former drinking of that whiskey or the smoking of those cigarettes or the using of those drugs because they have pointed up to you the obstacle in your soul which needs removal. Anything which helps you to learn more about yourself and your soul's needs is beneficial and should be blessed.

Once you come to see that whatever it is which you feel has dominion over you—even if it is another person—is merely a guidepost directing you toward discovering your true self, you have no choice except to bless it. It is at this initial point of blessing that its grip on you will begin loosening because you have now recognized it for what it is: an area in you which needs attention.

CONCERN FOR ANOTHER PERSON

Your loved one's problem has presented you with a wonderful opportunity to grow. No matter how bleak the situation appears, there is good in it for him and for you. You cannot release his good for him but you can release your own. And you do so by blessing the situation, by freeing yourself of it and not allowing it to affect you further.

The step of blessing a person who appears to be in the midst of a challenge is the most effective thing you can do for him. In fact, it is really the *only* thing you can do for him!

This releases you from making his problem your problem. And it directs loving, supportive, healing energies toward the person which he may be able to utilize in his own soul's growth.

You will find much peace once you can genuinely bless and release that challenge which your loved one is facing and which you were letting affect you. Blessing benefits the blesser as well as the blessed.

THINGS TO DO

I)   Consider in what way your particular problem is a blessing to you. Write a paragraph or two on it. This is important!

II)   Decide how you can bless your problem.

   A) Compose a *meaningful* blessing that you can say whenever you think of the situation which is troubling you. Make it short—something that is easy to remember.

   B) Memorize this blessing.

III)   Put a definite time aside each day to actively bless the situation or person troubling you.

   A) If you are having trouble blessing a person, try to see the "sign" hanging around his or her neck which reads "Please, Love Me." Bring this image into your meditation each day. *See* that sign blinking brightly and know that his request for love is always there and that it comes from a deep soul thirst which cannot be *fully* quenched until you love him.

B) Image the person not as he looks now but as he looked when he was an infant. See him as the pure, innocent guileless baby that he was. It is easy to love a baby. The more strongly you can image this person as a baby, the more easily it will be to love him. Eventually you will be seeing the perfect Christ of that baby. Since you know that the Christ is *always* in us, it will be easy to transfer that love to the person as he is today, loving him from your perfect Christ-center to his perfect Christ-center.

Lesson Four

COMMITMENT

To be used in conjunction with Chapter VI of the Text.

Are you ready to make a *total* commitment to your goal? A real, all-out, no-holds-barred commitment? If you feel you are ready to make such a commitment it means that you are ready to enter into a solemn, binding contract with God! God becomes your partner in your SOUL SURGERY.

You should know that God is more than willing to enter into a covenant with you because God can only work *for* you when He can work *with* you.

Many people fail in their efforts to heal a situation or condition because they are not willing to enter into a *total* commitment with God. They are aware of the need for a solution and they even bless the problem, but they lack the zeal which can motivate them to direct their energies towards achieving their goal.

To be commited to your goal means that you see with the "single eye." Your entire life is directed to your goal.

Everything you think, say and do will support that commitment. You will do as Jesus did when "He steadfastly set His face to go to Jerusalem," when He *knew* what He had to do and would not let anyone or anything change his direction.

There comes a time when we finally get in tune with the Infinite, when we decide to listen to the Christ in us and make the decision of a special overcoming. In each of us there is a Jerusalem which we know we must meet with trust and total commitment. Whatever we "set our face" to do, we can do. But it must involve our whole being. It is this kind of dedication which is necessary for you to make now, and a covenant verbalizes this commitment and helps to focus your energies on it. It elevates you from a feeling of being in tune with the *indefinite* to an assurance of being in tune with the *infinite*.

And so you will write a covenant.

HEALTH

Do you *really* want to get rid of your sickness? If so, then make a strong commitment to health. Your commitment will mirror your desire.

Sit down and write a well thought-out covenant between you and the life force dwelling in your body. Acknowledge this indwelling life force as the power which makes you well. Then make specific promises to obey the laws of health, nutrition and exercise and to keep a positive mental attitude. Promise to do all you can on your own behalf, knowing that as long as you do your share the life force within you will respond and reward you with the health and wholeness that you desire.

Put this convenant in a conspicuous place so that you see it daily and will be kept motivated to honor your commitment.

Next, image yourself whole and healthy. Project the image of health that you desire onto your mind. See yourself *exactly* the way you want to be—whole and healthy, free of pain and perfect in every way. Whenever you think of yourself let it be in this image. You are healthy. Imagine it!

An extremely hypertensive accountant wrote and signed a covenant after suffering a mild stroke. In addition to general promises to change his consciousness and to seek God's help more, were very *specific* promises to walk to the train station each day, change his poor eating habits and to stop smoking.

You can receive proper guidance through meditation. This guidance will help you to have a better idea of the steps which you should include in your covenant.

It could even be that at this particular time you are guided to seek medical assistance with your problem. If so, then that would be included in your covenant too. The life force responds to medication as well as meditation. Follow your inner guidance and decide for yourself.

PROSPERITY

Make a promise NOW to do something about your poverty. Plan your actions. Write them down. Exactly what are you going to do about your poverty? Writing out a plan will help to motivate you into following that plan. You know that infinite abundance flows from only one Source. Make a covenant with that Source, promising to do all you can to allow It to flow through you.

Image yourself prosperous and successful. Let this picture of a prosperous you be your *constant* image of yourself. Never think of yourself as a "poor" person or a "needy" person. You are prosperous!

There is one very specific promise which should be included in your covenant if you wish to attain a prosperity consciousness, and that is your *commitment to giving*. It should be stated very definitely that you promise to lovingly give at every opportunity.

The only way to receive is to first give. By writing a covenant which you will read each day, you gradually impress your subconscious mind with the truth of that statement. Find specific things to do which will help open up that flow of infinite abundance which surrounds you.

Perhaps your covenant might include tithing or some other type of financial commitment. But be sure to include love as the attitude in which you give. This is important. In fact, this is *crucial!* We don't give with an attitude of receiving. We give because it is our nature to be like God, who is always giving. As a "side effect" of our giving, of course, we free ourselves to receive and we will receive in abundance.

PERSONAL RELATIONSHIPS

Make a commitment to love. It's not unnatural. In fact, loving is the most natural thing that you can do! When there is a serious conflict with another you may find it very difficult to show any love; this is understandable. Too often we all let our ego-inflated sense consciousness get in the way of our ego-free spiritual consciousness and we judge the motives of others more severely than we would want to be judged ourselves. For this reason, because it is often so difficult to love others, it is very important to make a formal commitment to do so. This wil tend to motivate you more than would a vague desire.

Sit down right now and write out a covenant with God, Infinite Love, promising to make a concerted effort to allow love to flow through you to those who stand in conflict with you. When you honor your part of the covenant—that is, love—God will honor His part and you will be loved. It can be no other way; it is the Law.

Imagination can play a big part in helping you to love more fully. If loneliness is your problem, envision yourself loving all and being loved by all. *Feel* the love flowing from you to everyone you meet and *feel* it flowing back to you from everyone. If you feel hatred toward someone or someone feels hatred toward you, *see* his Christ center. Don't think of him as a flesh and blood enemy but as a spiritual brother. Love him from Christ center to Christ center and *see* the love going from your Christ center to his Christ center—from your perfect essence to his perfect essence. Practice this envisioning. If you have trouble seeing his Christ center through all the debris of hatred, imagine how he looked when he was one month old, or six months old or a year old. It is easy to see the perfect spiritual essence of an infant and it is only a small step to transfer those feelings to the adult.

What *specific* things can you do which will help heal your relationship? Remember that your covenant is between you and God. It involves only *your* part in the relationship problem—not the other person. So be sure that your covenant lists only those things which *you* will do.

Be very specific. It is much more effective to say that you will take a certain action like actively affirming love for the mother-in-law who has been making life so miserable for you than it is for you to say you will be loving in general. Not that you should not be loving at all times, but the purpose of the covenant is to get yourself to focus on a *specific* action that you can take each day. For example, to make a *specific* commitment to take time each day to listen patiently to your troublesome teenaged daughter who is just entering into young womanhood, which is confusing and bewildering to her, is a much more meaningful commitment than a commitment simply to be "understanding" or "loving."

What *specific* steps are you willing to take to harmonize your unhappy relationship? Give a lot of thought to your covenant before actually writing it. Clarify your goal and specify your actions.

And, of course, don't forget to put God first in any relationship.

DOMINION

Commitment is one of the most important areas in dealing with problems of dominion. You must *keep yourself motivated* at all times so that you don't give up if results are not immediately to your satisfaction.

Problems of dominion are usually a long time in developing. If results are not immediate it is usually because you are having trouble changing your consciousness to conform to your new wishes. A well thought-out covenant, listing *specific* things you want dissolved from your life and *specific* things you will do to dissolve them, is an invaluable motivator.

Make a covenant today. Write it out and post it on your bathroom mirror so that you will see it daily and be reminded daily of your commitment.

An attorney with a drinking problem made a fine covenant which motivated him to follow through with his SOUL SURGERY. He included such specific steps as joining a support group (in this case Alcoholics Anonymous), learning how to correct his diet, and ceremoniously clearing his home and office of alcohol (and clearing his lifestyle of cocktail parties and bars!).

In the case of dominion it is best to write as strongly-worded a covenant as you can, then post it in a conspicuous place where you will read it at least twice a day.

Be sure to include God as your silent, faithful partner in your covenant. When you are consciously aware that you are heir to all of His gifts and love you cannot possibly be dominated by anything or anyone. Refer to this truth in your covenant and that you are relying on God as your ever-present support system.

CONCERN FOR ANOTHER PERSON

It may be difficult at times to keep from interfering in a loved one's problem. It's natural to want to help someone you love. But you must remember that the best help you can render is to see the Christ—the perfect center—of him. You can do no better than to hold this image. You can help yourself do this by writing out a reminder to yourself, stating the consequences of personal interference and the rewards of positive envisioning. Post it in a conspicuous place where it will prompt you to keep yourself centered so that your thinking remains focused on Spirit.

How would you write a covenant in this case? First remember that your only responsibility is to lovingly hold the other person in a perfect light and see him as perfect—not necessarily the way *you* want him to be but the way *God* wants him to be. "Not my will but Thine be done."

Put a lot of thought into what specific things you will do. It is very likely that the problem is you! You are really dealing with *your* reactions to the other person's problem. Don't write the covenant enumerating the things that *he* should do, word your covenant to motivate *you* to release the person to work out his own good.

This is a situation which requires constant contact with your perfect center—your Christ self—in order to stay on course and to receive proper guidance and strength. Make a commitment to regular, daily meditation a clause in your covenant. Also helpful is a regular daily meditation drill of holding the person in the perfect light and seeing him as perfect and happy. Imagine your loved one free of any problem. See him clearly in your mind. Hold the image of that perfect center of him—his Christ center. Every time you think of him let it be in this way. The power of imagination is a very real power and is so important when we are concerned for another.

THINGS TO DO

You must now write out your covenant. The following is an example of a typical covenant. Naturally you will adapt it to your own needs, but you might want to stay with this general form.

"Creative Power of the Universe, I know that You are present in my life and my affairs. I know that You are in the midst of this present challenge and that I have only to maintain a sense of my oneness with You in order to let Your good flow freely through me.

"I know that when I operate from my perfect center and make an appropriate effort on my own behalf, You will always be there to put Your strength behind my effort—supporting, guiding, directing and assisting me.

"Therefore on this _____ day of _____, 19 _____, I freely, joyfully and with complete faith make this covenant with You.

"I promise to _____.
"I promise to _____.
"I promise to _____.

"I unhesitatingly enter into this covenant with You, God. I am resolute in my commitment to change my life and am absolutely secure in the knowledge that as long as I honor my commitment You will honor Yours and that my life will overflow with Your abundant gifts.

"Signed _____"

The very act of writing your covenant will motivate and fill you with enthusiasm. It has forced you to examine your situation very carefully and to seek inner guidance. You have now "set your face to Jerusalem" and are prepared to make a total commitment to achieving your goal. You have made a sacred covenant between you and God. You cannot fail. All you have to do is to honor your part of the contract; you know God will honor His.

Lesson Five

DENIALS & AFFIRMATIONS

To be used in conjunction with Chapter VII of the Text.

The technique of denials and affirmations is so basic and deceptively simple that it is easy to disregard it, forgetting how very effective it can be. But we need these powerful tools when we are undertaking SOUL SURGERY.

Denials are a tearing-down process. They destroy and remove the negative aspects from our soul—those beliefs and ideas and attitudes which are not based on Truth.

Affirmations are a building-up process. They construct and implant the positive aspects of our spirit—those beliefs and ideas and attitudes which are based on Truth.

Have you already been working with denials and affirmations? If so, perhaps you can improve upon them. If not, it is time to incorporate them into your SOUL SURGERY.

HEALTH

Deny the inevitability of sickness in your life. You may not at this time be able to deny the "reality" of sickness—

after all, you do feel pain and discomfort. But you can deny its power over you and you can deny its inevitability. You did not inherit that sickness from the life force within you. The life force knows nothing of pain and sickness. It knows only life and seeks only life.

The Truth of your being is that you are *in essence* perfect. Sickness has no part in your perfect plan. In God's realm there is no sickness. Your denials and affirmtions, therefore, must reflect this Truth if they are to work.

You could use a denial such as, "I do not inherit sickness," or "I no longer need sickness in my life," or "I no longer restrict the flow of the life force through my body," or any similar statement which denies the error of your fear and the false appearances of the condition.

Your affirmation might be something like, "I am perfect," or "God is healing me now," or "I allow the life force to express a perfect body," or whatever appeals to you to affirm *just so it is based on Truth.*

Be sure to have at least one denial and one affirmation memorized—one that is very meaningful to you. Each time a thought of fear or discouragement arises, substitute for that thought at once with your denial and/or affirmation.

PROSPERITY

Experience a change of consciousness. You can receive prosperity in your life *only to the extent that your consciousness can accept it!* Expand your limited poverty consciousness to an unlimited prosperity consciousness. Begin conditioning your consciousness by denying that poverty has any place in your life. You no longer need it, so why keep it? Whatever purpose it has served is no longer valid or you would not want to take specific steps to rid yourself of it.

"I no longer need poverty in my life."

"Any poverty consciousness I may have had is now dissolved forever."

Use affirmations to prepare your consciousness to accept your prosperity.

"I demonstrate success and prosperity in my life and affairs."

"All of my needs are met."

"I am rich and prosperous in every way."

PERSONAL RELATIONSHIPS

If you walk outside on a sunny day with your eyes closed you will be in the dark, but has the sun stopped shining? Of course not. The sun has been blocked by your eyelids but it is still shining!

If there is a lack of love in your life it is only because you have closed your eyes to it. Lack of love does not exist in creation—hatred, loneliness, and unloving relationships are not real and can have no power in your life. Deny the appearance of the negative situation in which you find yourself.

"There is no hatred in my life or affairs."

"No one is unloved in God's universe."

"I no longer need hatred or loneliness."

Affirm the reality, which is that as soon as you "open your eyes" to the love all around you it will flow through you and to you.

"I open my eyes to the infinite love which abounds."

"I am loving."

"I am loved."

DOMINION

Very strong denials and affirmations are usually particularly effective in the case of dominion. The Truth that you are made in the image and likeness of God and that *you cannot be held in bondage to anything or anyone* must be the basis of your thinking. However, because you may have allowed yourself to be dominated for so long, you may have forgotten this elementary fact. Whenever the temptation arises to put yourself back in bondage remind yourself by uttering, either silently or audibly, a meaningful denial like "this (situation, person or thing) has no power in my life" or "I am not in bondage to this or to anything," or even "I no longer need this in my life."

Make up your own denial. Make it meaningful to you and say it *with conviction* throughout the day. It will help to remind you of the Truth.

Just as important as denying that which is false is affirming that which is true—"You shall know the truth and the truth shall make you free." Condition your consciousness with meaningful statements of Truth such as "There is only one power in my life—God," or "I have been given dominion over *all* things," or "I am free."

Use these affirmations to build a state of mind based on Truth. They will help to mold the attitudes and ideas which mold your life and affairs.

CONCERN FOR ANOTHER PERSON

Denials and affirmations are so important when dealing with the actions of others. It is so easy to be swayed by how things appear instead of how they are in Truth. It's very easy to be affected by what others do. That's why denials and affirmations are so valuable; they help weed out these erroneous beliefs and plant positive attitudes.

And you must be very careful to word your denials and affirmations so that they call upon God's will, not yours. The soul of the other person has to work out its own problems and you must never interfere, for that would impede *your* progress.

Your denials and affirmations in this situation should be based on the Truth that only God knows what is best for each person. As much as you might love this special person, your denials and affirmations must reflect only that there is no Truth to this person's unhappiness and that he is a Christ-filled creature.

Your denial, therefore, could be "These appearances are not the real Truth of John's life," or "I will not react negatively to Mary's struggle."

Your affirmation could be, "I see through appearances to the perfection of John," or "Mary is steadily recognizing her perfection," or simply "I see my son as perfect." In other words, you are to only affirm perfection and must never use affirmations to try to change the other person to fit your mold. Do you see the difference? It is an important distinction.

Situations like this are often more difficult for us than working on ourselves. We should always make certain that our denials and affirmations conform to the bounds of our own responsibility, which is to see only joy and perfection in the other person. In that way we are not trying to interfere with his soul growth.

THINGS TO DO

Make up your own denial and affirmation. One good, strong denial and one powerful affirmation based on Truth is all you really need. They can be easily memorized and called upon during the day when needed.

DENIALS usually have the most appeal to those who remember vividly and tend to dwell on the past—especially past troubles. Also those who tend to be more aggressive and self-confident usually find denials very meaningful and tend to rely on them more than affirmations.

AFFIRMATIONS usually are more meaningful to those who are timid and fearful, who feel that their lives are ineffective and who "give in" easily. Affirmations also appeal to those who are doubting and anxious or who are passive and lack confidence.

Whichever technique is more meaningful to you, don't use it exclusively. Both denials and affirmations should be used, although it is acceptable to use one more than the other.

Make your statements short and vivid. And they are much more effective when they are your own. Once in a while you may find someone else's denial or affirmation which strikes a responsive chord in you, but usually the ones you yourself make up are more meaningful and therefore more powerful. Remember, denials and affirmations are tools to expand your consciousness. They are ''spiritual training wheels'' to help you until you find your divine equilibrium. They must have a strong meaning for you in order to be effective.

I)   Make up three strong, true and meaningful DENIALS appropriate to your situation.

    1.

    2.

    3.

II) Make up three powerful, true and positive AFFIRMATIONS appropriate to your situation.

    1.

    2.

    3.

III) Now select the one DENIAL and the one AFFIRMATION which have the most meaning for you.

    1. My DENIAL is:

    2. My AFFIRMATION is:

IV) Memorize them both.

V) Repeat them often—silently, or audibly when possible —until they become so much a part of you that they spring to mind automatically. That is when they do their best work of impressing your consciousness with the truth of your present challenge.

Lesson Six

EFFORT

To be used in conjunction with Chapter VIII of Text.

All of the steps of your SOUL SURGERY so far have been involved with consciousness—with your thinking and feeling faculties. This is as it should be. All things begin in the mind, with ideas and beliefs.

You have become AWARE of exactly what your challenge is and, hopefully, what the ultimate cause of it is. You are able to BLESS the situation because it contains the seed of your good. You made a solemn COMMITMENT in the form of a covenant with God which is motivating you towards achieving your goal. And you are using those wonderful soul conditioners, DENIALS and AFFIRMATIONS, to bring about a change of consciousness. *Now is the time to take action!* It is time to bring the new ideas and new attitudes out into the physical world. It is time to show God (and yourself) that you mean business! And the only way you can do this is by making an effort—a genuine effort—on your own behalf.

Without an effort all of the groundwork which you have laid up to this point will dissipate into wisps of whimsy, accomplishing little or nothing. No matter how sincere or extensive your first four steps of SOUL SURGERY might be, if they aren't going to culminate into a dedicated effort they haven't been successful. The degree of your own inner conviction will reflect in the degree of effort which you are now willing to put forth. Your effort thus becomes the outward proof of your inner dedication. It is your tangible assurance to God that you believe in yourself—and in Him.

HEALTH

You will discover there are numerous efforts you can make on behalf of the life force within you. By seeking your inner guidance you will be shown what these efforts can be. Of course, you will begin by making an effort to stop condemning your body with your thoughts and words. The healing and renewing life force is denied to all who dwell on their maladies and freely flows in all who praise their health.

Important, too, is obeying the laws of health. Should you really expect to get over diabetes while still living on cola drinks and sugared doughnuts? (Remember that God dwells in the foods that *He* made, not in *man's* perversions of the food that He made!) Is it reasonable to expect improvement in your heart if you refuse to exercise and lose weight? Does it make sense to pray for help with emphysema as long as you are still smoking? The laws of nutrition, exercise and healthful living are just as valid as any other laws. All are part of the law of cause and effect. If the "cause" is inferior food and lack of exercise the "effect" will be inferior health.

If you desire health you must act on your own behalf. Make a meaningful effort to help yourself. Become involved and put a deed behind your desire.

Your effort might even involve seeking medical help. The life force works through prayer and medication as well as through prayer and meditation. Or it could involve taking vitamin and mineral supplements. An important thing to realize is that once you begin directing your attention to making an all-out effort for your health, you will be flooded with ideas and alternatives.

PROSPERITY

If *you* don't act on your own behalf, who will? If you want to demonstrate more prosperity then *you* are going to have to do something about it. Only you can work to better yourself. You can't be successful if you are like the very talented writer who only wrote when he was "inspired." Unfortunately for him he was inspired only a few hours a week and never did become a success.

A desire takes a doing. You cannot be successful and prosperous without effort. That would be expecting something for nothing.

Get to work doing something about your own success NOW. The sooner you begin, the sooner you can experience the prosperity you desire and deserve.

And don't forget about giving. No matter how dire you feel your financial circumstances are at this time, give *something* of what you have, no matter how small in quantity.

The action of giving lovingly produces dramatic results. Once you freely give—*without a sense of losing something*—you will have advanced yourself into a state of prosperity.

PERSONAL RELATIONSHIPS

What effort can you make to help create peace, happiness and love? What action could you take to help bring God's will for perfection into manifestation? It will require meditation to receive guidance as to your efforts. Although actions will vary from one individual circumstance to another, the basic underlying effort has to be anchored in love, understanding and total non-judgment. When so anchored, *all* efforts will then spring from your perfect center and you will never have to ask yourself, "Am I doing the right thing?" The Christ within will always guide you correctly.

Don't ask, "How can I be loved?" That is putting last things first! We love *first* and then we are loved. All love follows our efforts to love. *If we want to be loved we must first love.*

Begin today, begin right now, to turn your life around. Make an effort to love those in conflict with you. Love them from your center to their center. Try as hard as you can to keep focused on that perfect essence of them no matter how hard they try to cover it up. Make every effort to mentally embrace them with all the love you are capable of expressing. Don't worry if you have trouble doing it when you begin. After all, the most proficient pianist struggled playing the simplest scales when he began. The important thing is the effort. As long as you keep striving you will improve. The more you love the more you can love and the more you can love the more you will be loved.

You can see the need, then, for frequent contact with your Source. It is when you act apart from your true self, when you want "*my* will" instead of "*Thy* will," that you run into difficulty. Always return to your Source for instructions and inspiration and you can never go wrong. Your effort will always be directed toward the good of all concerned.

DOMINION

By now you might already have been making some effort to win your freedom. Are there additional actions you can see the need for? Attaining your goal is going to require persistent effort, so it is important to decide what that effort will be. Without effort there can be no improvement. A desire without a deed is surely a dead-end. *You* must make an attempt to improve yourself. *You* must do something about your condition. No one can stop smoking for you or drinking for you or overeating for you. In the final analysis *you* must do it yourself. And the key to acting on your own behalf when dealing with such longstanding problems is to live in the NOW. Don't worry about what you did in the past or how you will act in the future. Don't have that drink NOW, don't smoke that cigarette NOW, don't eat that rich dessert NOW. To envision the rest of your life without another drink or another cigarette or another piece of pie may seem too much to bear, but to think only of not having one NOW is something you can deal with. Don't try to live three hundred and sixty-five days at a time. Don't even try to live twenty-four hours at a time. Live in the NOW and act in the NOW!

Everything you have done up to this point has been to prepare yourself to make a concerted effort on your own behalf. God will help you, certainly. But God can not do *for* you, God can only do *through* you.

Will your effort involve not touching alcohol, or drugs, or tobacco or wrong foods? Will it mean dealing with another person on a Christ-to-Christ basis rather than a slave-to-master basis?

Will it mean joining a support group such as Alcoholics Anonymous or Gamblers Anonymous or Overeaters Anonymous?

What specific actions are you going to follow? Are you prepared to carry them out determinedly and dedicatedly? And what if you falter and slide back on occasion? Are you serious enough about your SOUL SURGERY to pick yourself up and go forward again, undaunted and free of guilt?

Follow your inner wisdom when deciding on your plan of action. And once you receive your guidance, ACT on it!

CONCERN FOR ANOTHER PERSON

Perhaps the greatest and most important (and often the most difficult) effort you can make on behalf of someone else is to make no effort at all! In other words, your effort would be to restrain yourself from taking any action which, no matter how "justified" or "helpful" it might seem, would interfere with that person's soul growth.

It requires great effort to keep from imposing your unsolicited "help" on another. Your duty is to be loving, understanding and supportive and to see that person as perfect. Your action can be in the form of prayer for that person's highest good (God's idea of good—not necessarily yours) and to envision him as happy and peaceful.

By following your inner guidance you will keep on the right track. You will be led to a loving release and then all of your concerns about your loved one will disappear as you place him back into the hands of God.

THINGS TO DO

I) Review the list of promises in your covenant.

    A) Do you still feel they are a valid way of overcoming your problem? Scrutinize the steps. Are they the best course of action for *all* involved?

    B) Are they realistic? Will you be able and willing to follow them every day? It is fine to tell yourself you will work at becoming healthier by exercising two hours every day, but is this realistic? Will it adapt to your lifestyle or will you do it for a few days and then drop it? It may be more realistic and practical to promise to exercise 20 minutes each morning and then walk to work or to the train station instead of driving.

    C) Are the steps specific enough to follow? Remember, in order to accomplish your goal, you must take *specific* actions. It may not be enough merely to promise to love a neighbor who has been a problem. A more specific deed would be to invite her over for lunch or to the next backyard barbecue or to make any other overt act of love and kindness toward her. An affirmative action will convince not only your neighbor but also you, yourself, of the depth of your commitment to loving her.

D) Lastly, and most importantly, are you following them daily? Regularity is the key. Sporadic actions on your own behalf can only lead to unsatisfactory results.

II) Meditate daily to maintain contact with your inner awareness so that you have constant guidance in your efforts and can change your program to suit the constantly improving you.

III) Get started NOW. Don't wait another day!

Lesson Seven

FAITH

To be used in conjunction with Chapter IX of Text.

Not only do we need to have faith in God as the Source of all good, but we also need to have complete faith in our ability to make contact with and receive that good. To have faith we must believe that *all is good*. To maintain our faith we must keep out of our thoughts anything which is contrary to that truth.

Spiritual Substance is everywhere around you, just waiting to be used by you for your good. The good is already there, otherwise it would be impossible to ever attain it, no matter how you tried. But your fear can keep your good from you. Fear is an insidious barrier obstructing your good.

And yet what is fear? Simply faith used in the wrong way.

You have unlimited faith within you. How are you investing that faith? Where are you putting it? Are you placing it on your problem, thereby giving that problem more power, or are you placing it on your deliverance—on God?

It is vital for you to know that where your faith is there will be your power *and* your results. It is just that simple.

HEALTH

Re-read the true stories of the girl at Lourdes and the man using the drug krebiozen. See how each outcome precisely followed the direction of the faith involved.

Carefully examine your own faith. Where will your faith lead? Is it focused on the appearance of some false condition or is it fixed on the Truth, which is that you are perfect because the Creative Force of the Universe dwells within you?

If you really believe that the life force within you can do its perfect work, you will not be fearful or upset at what appears to be the opposite of this. *Know* that the truth is more powerful—superior in every way—to any appearance of disease or disharmony in the body. Don't just think it, *know* it. You are dealing with Law. Law is not capricious. Have faith in it, *believe* you have received it and you will.

PROSPERITY

It's very easy to have faith in something we've already experienced. If your challenge is in the area of prosperity you are very fortunate because your effort at *freely* and *lovingly* giving should already be proving to you the great Truth that God's abundance is unlimited.

Once you get into the flow of this good—this abundance —you will be demonstrating greater and greater prosperity. The more you demonstrate, the stronger your faith will become. And the stronger your faith, the more you will prosper!

Keep your faith on God's good, which is yours to use. Do not make the mistake of thinking that your new demonstrations of abundance are mere coincidences or just a bit of good luck. Never! Your abundance is a direct result of your correct use of God's law. You freely and lovingly give and so you prosper. Keep your faith on that law and your prosperity will amaze you.

Remember not to expect to always reap where you have sown. Your good can come from any direction. Your faith therefore must be centered on the good, on God, and never on the material channel which will provide it.

Your faith in God's abundance will soon be carried over into all areas of your life, for the same abundance can flow freely as health, harmony, peace and love. Isn't that exciting? That's why true giving serves to connect you with your Creator, keeping you in contact with Spirit.

PERSONAL RELATIONSHIPS

Have you been secretly fearing or believing that this situation will never resolve itself or come out well? If so, you have been pouring your faith into negativity and undesirable results.

God is in charge of your situation! Do you *really* believe that? If you do, then your faith will be held on the perfect solution for everyone involved. All of your efforts—both physical and mental—will be directed towards good because it is your faith which is providing the mold, the channel, in which God can express.

When your faith is firmly rooted on the side of God it becomes much easier to work with the other steps of your SOUL SURGERY. As soon as your faith is placed where it belongs, God's perfect plan can begin to unfold.

DOMINION

Dominion is a clear-cut case of misplaced faith. You have believed that distilled spirits or drugs or tobacco or another of God's creatures can have some say in determining your life. You have had faith in the ability of someone or something to control your destiny.

That same power of faith which you had projected in the wrong direction will now be turned around and directed towards the Truth—towards God.

Each time you feel your faith dropping toward the bottom rung of "thinking and feeling," lift it immediately to the top rung of "knowing." *When you change the position of your faith, you will change the condition of your life.*

Another benefit arises. The more you proceed with your operation of SOUL SURGERY, the more you will be aware of changes and improvement. And this improvement will serve to keep your faith strongly on God.

Change the position of your faith and you will change your condition from bondage to liberty.

CONCERN FOR ANOTHER PERSON

Some steps of SOUL SURGERY are more easily accomplished in certain areas than others. Some steps require more work. Faith is such a step when related to helping another. It is here that firm faith is going to have to be one of your strongest steps.

If you truly want God's highest good for that person, you are going to have to show this by investing your faith in that good. This means that you cannot believe that any disease or way of life or mental attitude can destroy the person's life. It means that your faith must be securely anchored in the conviction that God dwells within him and is going to guide him towards his good.

The importance of right faith in this situation cannot be over-emphasized. Check out your own faith. Where does it lie? Regular meditation will help you to be aware of God's infinite presence and power and wisdom. This awareness will help you to keep your faith where it should be—on your perfection and on the perfection of your loved one.

God is most assuredly working in and through this other person. Believe that. Have faith in that truth.

THINGS TO DO

I)   Continually be on guard. *Watch for the signs which would indicate that you are misdirecting your faith.*

    A) Do you have fears, doubts and worries about the outcome of your problem?

    B) Do you often discuss your problem with others?

    C) Do you say such things as "my arthritis," or "I'll never be able to afford that," or "If only John would see what he is doing to his life"?

These are signs of misplaced faith. They are a warning to you to realign your faith with Truth.

II)   Consciously redirect your faith. Move it immediately back to God whenever you catch it going in the wrong direction. The more you work at doing this, the easier it becomes. Your affirmations can be of great help in accomplishing this.

III) Each evening take a mental tally of your faith investments for the day. Were most of them on the asset (positive) side or were there more on the debit (negative) side? Add them up and see which side has the larger total. While it is true that every wrong investment hurts and every right investment helps, the overall picture decides which side you're on. Whichever side contains more than fifty percent of the total will be the side which will produce the end result. Also, the higher the percentage on the plus side, the faster and stronger will be the arrival of God's good. (By the same law, the higher percentage on the minus side, the faster and stronger will be the arrival of the wrong answer!)

What is your score? Do the daily totals indicate that your faith is invested in fear or in God? Work at improving your score.

Lesson Eight

GOD'S TURN

To be used in conjunction with Chapter X of Text.

You have arrived at the final step of your SOUL SUR-GERY. It is possible that during your operation you may have found that a certain step did not seem important or even necessary to your success. If so, that is perfectly acceptable and understandable.

But no matter what steps you took or how you used them, you cannot fully attain your goal without taking the final step of letting God have His turn. In fact, we could even say that the only important step, the perfect answer to any situation, is really GOD'S TURN— God's will, God's divine plan for us.

Whatever the problem, whatever the challenge, God must be permitted His turn because He needs that turn in order to bring the answer to you. Does God always have the answer? Not only does He *have* the answer—He *IS* the answer!

Your other six steps of SOUL SURGERY are all paving the way for God to take His perfect turn. You are conscientiously doing your share and now God can do His.

HEALTH

If you are faithfully carrying out your part of the operation, it must follow that God will carry out His. When you are certain that you are doing all that you can do (and you must examine your own consciousness for this), then it is time to release the situation to God so that He can work out the perfect means of bringing about your healing.

But the release must be complete. There can be no hanging onto any false appearances which might still be present or any symptoms which still may persist. God will take care of these in His own time and in His own way.

Once you turn the situation over to God there must be no checking up on things "to see if it's working." Release and let go. God is your health. God is working out your healing now. If you can honestly say that you've done your share, then there is not a chance in the world that you will not be able to accept God's good.

Let God have His turn and prepare to accept your healing now.

PROSPERITY

God's desire for you is unlimited prosperity and happiness. As soon as you began using your other six steps of SOUL SURGERY you were clearing the way for God to have His turn so that He could freely pour His abundance into your life.

Once this abundance begins to flow, do not interrupt it by trying to take matters back into your own hands with doubts, questions and fears. Are you lovingly and freely giving of your good to others? Do you give without fear of loss? Do you give with no strings attached? If your answer to these questions is an honest "yes," you can confidently turn things over to God and He will prosper you.

God is your financial partner. But His abundance will find its way into all areas of your life. When God takes His turn you will prosper in health, love, peace and joy because God cannot withhold part of His good once you let Him express through you.

Completely release your finances to God and prepare to accept His prosperity now. You have nothing to lose but your lack!

PERSONAL RELATIONSHIPS

There is no relationship problem that God cannot resolve. When you are working with God, you are working with the Law and the Law is not fickle. When you do your share the Law—or God—does Its share. All you have to do is to let go. You have engaged the gears of your good, now just let them turn.

Let God have His turn. Let Him reveal His marvelous plan for you. Continue doing your share, but do it in the full expectation that God is at work using your SOUL SURGERY to bring forth your solution. All is well. God is here. Be prepared to accept your peace, harmony and happiness now.

Show gratitude for your good although you may not yet see it. If you can give thanks *before* you see it, you have truly let go. "I am grateful for the abundance of love in my life."

DOMINION

Go back over each previous step of your SOUL SURGERY. Are you religiously doing each one? Is there any place where you could improve upon what you are doing? Is there any way in which you could do more of your share?

Take these questions into your meditation. Consider them prayerfully and repeatedly. If you are completely convinced that you are doing the very best you can, release the problem to God. Turn it over to Him so that He can put together all of the work you have been doing and fashion it into your true deliverance.

God is your ultimate support system. You can count on Him. You can lean on Him if you need to. Your first six steps of SOUL SURGERY are *your* contribution to your freedom. You now must turn it over to God so that He can make *His* contribution. God always is more than ready to take His turn, but He can only do so after you have taken yours. You have, and so now He will. Prepare to accept your freedom now. The best way to do this is to give thanks. Gratitude indicates your assurance in your eventual good. "Free at last, free at last, thank God Almighty, I'm free at last."

Concern for Another Person

In the case of helping someone else your first six steps have all been in one way or another actually God's turn! You became *aware* that God is the answer. You are *blessing* the problem because God is at work in it. You made a *commitment* to let God's will be done. You *denied* anything which appears less than divine and you *affirmed* God's presence and perfect solution. Your *effort* is to see only God and to let God work through that soul. Your *faith* is in the truth that God knows what is best for this person and will perfectly work it out for him.

In reality is has been God's turn at every step of the way! Now use this seventh step to officially release the situation into God's hands. They can hold whatever you put into them.

Remember, when you are working with the steps of SOUL SURGERY you are working with Universal Law. The Law is scrupulously fair and impartial. If you are doing all that you can and are keeping your faith strong, how can you possibly fail? The only way that you can fail is if you won't release the problem from your life and give it over to the Universal Life Force—God. Let go of it right now! As you are working toward the solution know that the solution is working toward you just as steadily and just as surely.

When you completely turn things over to God you will experience a deep sense of joyful peace. Let God have His turn and prepare to accept your peace now.

THINGS TO DO

I) Make a routine check of all steps to be sure you are doing your share.

   A) Have you uncovered the *Ultimate Cause*—your soul's need—which created the problem?

   B) Are you still able to bless the situation as being the source of good for you?

   C) Do you daily read your covenant, letting it inspire and motivate you?

   D) Have your denials and affirmations become a real part of your consciousness?

   E) What effort are you making? Have you remained true to it? Are you doing your very best?

   F) Where is your faith invested? Are you working at centering it on God?

II) Is your Christ self satisfied with how you are proceeding with your SOUL SURGERY? Are you meditating daily to keep in contact with your Christ self?

III) Have you imposed a time limit on the solution of your problem? If so, this is an indication that you haven't yet let it go.

IV) Have you been able to say with deep feeling, "Thank you, Father, for my good," even if your good may not yet be manifest? If the answer is "yes," you have given your problem to God—it is truly GOD'S TURN. Relax and experience the peace that passes all understanding which comes from knowing that God is now taking His turn. No turning back now—only total release. Prepare to accept your highest good NOW.

ALL THINGS ARE POSSIBLE

Now you have completed your SOUL SURGERY. You have finally excised that malignant false belief which has been blocking the full expression of your innate perfection. You have achieved what God had planned for you from the start. You have taken God on as a partner and know now that "with God all things are possible" is more than a group of words—it is a truth which you have proven to yourself.

Should another challenge appear in your life, you know that you are not helpless in its clutches. No matter how hopeless it appears to be, you can always perform another operation, another SOUL SURGERY to remove it so that Spirit flows unimpededly once more.

What a comfort, what a joy to know that God is always the answer and that by simply removing all false beliefs from your soul you can attain the self-healing you are seeking. More importantly, however, your self-healing will have gotten you so very much closer to the realization of that ultimate state of self-perfection for which you were unmistakably created and for which your soul so fervently yearns: that of becoming a perfect expression of a perfect Creator.